mcf

How to Grow
as an
Illustrator

Michael Fleishman

ALLWORTH PRESS
NEW YORK

11   10   09   08   07   5   4   3   2   1

Published by Allworth Press
An imprint of Allworth Communications, Inc.
10 East 23rd Street, New York, NY 10010

Cover design by Derek Bacchus
Interior design by SR Desktop Services, Ridge, NY
Page composition/typography by SR Desktop Services, Ridge, NY
Cover and chapter title illustrations © 2007 Michael Fleishman

Library of Congress Cataloging-in-Publication Data
      Fleishman, Michael, 1951–
      How to grow as an illustrator / Michael Fleishman.
            p.   cm.
      Includes index.
      ISBN-13: 978-1-58115-479-5
      ISBN-10: 1-58115-479-8
      1. Commercial art—Vocational guidance.   2. Graphic arts—
Vocational guidance.   I. Title.

NC1001.F57   2007
741.6023—dc22

                                             2007012919

Printed in Canada

CONTENTS

Introduction

Recently, before she went out to give a lecture discussing her documentary film, *On A Roll*, my wife, a documentary filmmaker, asked me to brainstorm a bit. "How would *you* talk about *your* process?" she asked.

"It's a multilevel thing," I replied, "and it all starts with an irresistible idea."

An irresistible idea, indeed. To me, illustration is that irresistible idea. From my earliest recollections, my career path was always a given—I'd be doing the proverbial "something in art."

As a kid, I wasn't a particularly industrious or stellar student, nor was I any kind of an athlete. Art wasn't quite the immovable force, though; I loved music (and for some time, being in a rock 'n' roll band owned much of my young adulthood. But even that eventually took a backseat to art school).

Sometime after I got my degree and made my way into the working world, there was *the* conscious moment I declared, "No more non–art–related jobs!" and decided to launch my freelance career. That was scary and exhilarating at the same time. Could I make it just doing what I loved?

Years and mileage eventually determine whether or not you can keep a number of burners—professionally, personally—on and cooking simultaneously. But there is an ever present life challenge: *how* to sustain that heat. Put another way, not just how to survive, but how to thrive . . . how to *grow*.

Who This Book Is For

Do you draw every day? What about the pressure of drawing on demand? Illustration isn't something you do just when the urge strikes you. Paying the bills is nothing to scoff at, but are you confident that while your art may speak for itself, it also speaks for *you*? Talent, energy, and attitude aren't underrated, but do you do work you like (or better yet, love) . . . stuff you're truly excited about . . . does it bring you joy?

There is life—your life—just past the edge of the drawing board. Are you in it, and fully engaged? This book is for those folks immersed in their illustration who want to stay afloat—no, make that those who want to swim vigorously—not only in the fishbowl of the studio, but also in the big pool of the world.

Where This Book Will Take the Reader

How to Grow will help you understand the multilayered definition of being an "illustrator" (and what that means in today's market, culture, and society). We will ask you *what* you do (and look at *how* you do it), and then discuss the motivations and inspirations of *why*.

We'll look at the *when* and *where* of illustration, too. Physical space, metaphysical place; that whole ride-to-work thing—getting to work in real time and metaphorically.

It's not breaking rocks in the hot sun, but this is a job; it is work—it's best to understand that right up front. But it is a job I adore. Fun. And if it's not fun—if it doesn't satisfy you on some gut level—why do anything?

Good question. I know, I know, there's that little question of being an adult and meeting responsibilities. I'm going to assume you want to go beyond basic survival and live outside of your head, though. And that's where *How to Grow* will attempt to transport you.

What You'll See along the Way

What does the book cover? Chapters discuss the standard sequence of events: roots and inspirations, references and resources, education and starting out, professional development and transition, career maintenance and change. We look at how mechanical skills and conceptual chops facilitate design, process, and product.

The book examines lifestyle, your spot in the world at large (as well as your personal and professional communities), your place in the big picture. *How to Grow* examines the impact of failure, mistakes, and calamities (big and small; mental, emotional, and physical). We talk about the business of illustration—climate, marketing, and promotion; education from both sides of the teacher's desk. We discuss staying in the field one way or another, as well as getting out of the life gracefully (if that's the answer).

It's a book written for illustrators by an illustrator, with invaluable perspective and input from some fifty other illustrators (who were gracious with their information and generous with good advice).

What Happens When You Get There

I say "been there," "done that," "made it" should be statements of victories (small and large)—not mutterings of boredom or conceit. And "coulda," "woulda," "shoulda"? Hopefully, just muscle aches in our cosmic physiology.

Perhaps, like all noble endeavors, illustration process is indeed a path (and illustration product, our destination). *How to Grow* seeks to provide a road map offering many alternate routes with a common theme: that getting there is indeed half the fun.

HOW TO GROW AS AN ILLUSTRATOR

mcf

1

Evolution or Revolution?

*There's no other way I can imagine
functioning in life. There's nothing else
I'd want to do with my time but
make images.*

—RAY-MEL CORNELIUS,
ILLUSTRATOR

Why Choose Illustration?   Here's the first baseball analogy you'll find in this book. Heads up: It may not be the last, by the way—art and baseball being two of life's greatest, most joyful recreations. The late Ted Williams hit .406 in 1941. As of this writing, he was the last major league player to hit over .400. His teammate Dom DiMaggio (Joe's brother, thus someone in an intimate position to recognize a quality swing) called him the "greatest left-handed hitter [he'd] ever seen."

As I understand it, Ted Williams hated being called a "natural" hitter. That one word negated all the dedication and work ethic he poured into the art and science of hitting a baseball.

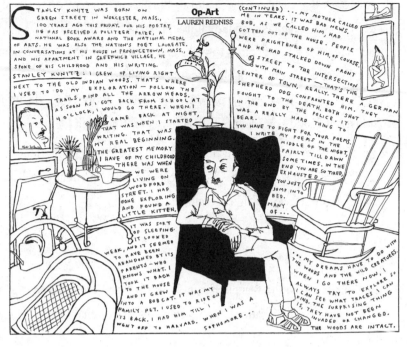

© Lauren Redniss

By that same token, no one is a "natural" or "born" illustrator, brought into this world with a Sharpie marker in his precious little fingers. I can't debate genetics (after all, I'm not a natural geneticist), but obviously, we are not blessed with the essential skill sets, knowledge base, or motor skills *at* birth (although it does make for a variety of interesting images).

This competence is usually acquired the old-fashioned way—the Ted Williams method: You learn it, you develop it, you sweat for it. For some of us it happens early—incredibly early in some cases (the latest child prodigy featured in *People* magazine). For others, growth is arrested at an early age (your friend who "can't even draw a straight line").

Our "born" illustrator taking his first arty-type baby steps (at whatever age) may not know a kernel of knowledge from a kernel of popcorn, but he knows instinctively that "I love this. I want to draw—gimme those crayons. I can't wait to finger paint today!"

It strikes me that early on, the "natural" illustrator inherently has a strong focus, a keen sense of the task, and a natural grasp of the rudiments. As a kid, no one had to teach me what colors to pick. Line quality was my middle name. Nobody made me go to my art table—I could effortlessly draw for hours at a time, even though I couldn't even pronounce the words "work ethic." From the get-go, it just felt "good" or "right." It was pure *fun*. It just felt like *me*.

As we get older, we qualify it differently; maybe we attach loftier labels to all this. Physically, it's not really a "job." Emotionally, spiritually, it "satisfies my soul." It's not "work," it's a "calling."

LABELS

I'd definitely make the wager that most illustrators live with an obsession for the practice of illustration. A particular intensity—that burn—to make art must be there.

"There are a couple of considerations," illustrator John Schmelzer tells us. "Are you a compulsive drawer? Do you just *have* to be drawing when listening to a lecture? How about that area to the left of the red line on a piece of lined paper? In your estimation, is this space made expressly for doodling?"

> *If you define yourself as an "illustrator" when asked what you do and you have the stomach to put up with the lousy hours, bad pay, and lack of respect that comes with the territory, you are probably suited to illustrate.*
> —JOHN SCHMELZER, ILLUSTRATOR

He goes on. "Do you think funny or different, or do your drawings make people laugh? Do your drawings help tell a story? Does a casual conversation inspire ideas, or can you grab a piece of it and use it as a departure point for a drawing? If so, you just may be an illustrator."

"To me," Ray-Mel Cornelius says, "the function of illustration has always been as a visual complement to another form of communication. It shouldn't be considered a subsidiary to that other form, but instead a copartner in the job of communicating."

"I don't see a difference between being an 'artist' and an 'illustrator,'" he continues. "In a broad sense, all art is illustration, particularly if it communicates an idea, emotion, experience, or thought process. And most art I'm aware of does this.

"The idea that illustration is by nature inferior to 'fine' or gallery art is a dead-horse argument. Art is either good or bad, on its merits, and even some illustration—even strictly functional illustration—can display creative and technical merit. By that same token, some illustration can be badly conceived and executed.

"I don't care about the perceived differences," Cornelius sums up, "but some others do, and that's unfortunate."

WELL, *IS* THERE A DIFFERENCE BETWEEN AN ARTIST AND AN ILLUSTRATOR?

Fine artist, illustrator . . . what's in a name? What's the big deal, anyway? Wouldn't one tag work just as well for the other?

If you must label, the concept of motivation will be one of the factors. If you need the discipline of solving a problem to make you draw, you very likely are an illustrator. "Plus, if you know exactly what you'll be paid before you start a project, then you probably qualify as well," Schmelzer adds. "I consider the likes of Michelangelo, da Vinci, Rembrandt, Sargent, Homer, and Eakins all to be illustrators in the modern definition."

Indeed. A famous illustrator, when asked to make the above evaluation, once said: "Frankly, my dear, I don't give a damn." Or maybe it was: "I know

Winslow Homer, sir—and you're no Winslow Homer!" Wait—I'm mixing my media here.

But Rhett's right (on both counts). You didn't miss the memo. For many of us, the difference between a "fine" artist and an "illustrator" is just mindset—pure semantics.

Higher and Deeper

So maybe it's this confusion over the *definition* of "illustration" and "art" (or "fine art") that has often led to contentious debate (and to more than a little misunderstanding). For, as illustrator and educator Bob Selby points out, "The difference between these terms is *not* a question of aesthetic opinion. Illustration (and its meaning) is a matter of English, not art."

Selby points out that these terms exist separately because they describe unique entities that are similar and often related. "However," Selby continues, "they are by no means aspects of the same thing.

"Neither will you find a picture of 'bad art' if you look up 'illustration' in the dictionary." Selby laughs. "The definition of illustration has nothing to do with quality."

The *Oxford English Dictionary* tells us that the term "illustration" springs from the Latin *illustrare*, meaning: "to light up, illuminate, or embellish." In its earliest usage, the term generally meant "enlightenment" in the spiritual sense.

The *American Heritage Dictionary* tells us that "illustrate" means: "(1a) To clarify, as by use of examples. (b) To serve as an instructive example of. (2) To provide (a publication) with explanatory or decorative graphic features."

But as Selby will tell you (working from this same source), "The term 'art,' on the other hand—also from Latin—means a 'creative or imaginative activity,' especially the expressive arrangement of elements within a medium.

"Despite the dictionary, there are probably as many definitions of art as there are artists," he muses, "and the matter is often debated. But the definition of illustration is consistent, if misunderstood. Common misuse is the culprit here, and clarity may lie in the philosophical roots of the two terms.

"Art just *is*," Selby states unequivocally. "A sculpture is. A painting is. There can be no question that these things exist as works of art. Without getting into further qualitative judgment, a work of art is a work of art—it is not a truck or a loaf of bread—it *is* art."

Illustration, on the other hand, does not require any such philosophical decisions. An illustration must recognize one certain requirement: Something must be in the condition of illustrating; it is being used to shed light. "There is action," Selby says. "In order to have illustration, something must be acting upon something else. There's no more to it than that, really."

Still with us here? Ultimately, this act of shedding light that we call "illustration" is a process Selby calls "symbolization." "We are enlightened—that is, we can know something—because illustrations function symbolically to shed their light on something else," Selby explains. "Drawings, for instance, can be tailored precisely to symbolize and, thereby, to highlight, clarify, amplify, complement, or explain something else."

The real deal is to enjoy the ride—that day-to-day act of being creative. This gets a little into a lifestyle thing, but there are other ways to make money—even more money, in fact. But are they as enjoyable? For me, being able to still create at the ripe old age of fifty-three is pretty neat.
—CHRIS SPOLLEN, ILLUSTRATOR

We should note then that the success or failure of illustration depends entirely upon *context*. How well does the painting, map, photograph, or chart function within its context to shed light on a subject is the ultimate test of illustration?

By that same token, when we frame and hang original N.C. Wyeth book paintings, we can only judge the work as fine art, because the paintings are no longer illustrating.

"Originals hanging in the Norman Rockwell Museum in Stockbridge, Massachusetts, are similar," Selby mentions. "We may refer to them as illustrations, but at this juncture it's only out of convenience. The framed originals in the museum are paintings, ontologically, and fine art to all those who consider them so. The fact that the work was originally created to illustrate is irrelevant."

Can this distinction work in the reverse? Sure. Frederick Remington originals could be said to shed light on life in the American West. Picasso's mural *Guernica* sheds light on inhumanity and the horrors of war. This powerful work of art presents history, geography, and psychology seminars on a monumental scale. In this context, Picasso's *Guernica* can indeed exist as an illustration.

"If you published a reproduction of the mural in the pages of a book on the Spanish Civil War, *Guernica* would be illustrating the text," Selby points out. "In that condition, the image of *Guernica* would be an illustration." The mural is art; the *use* of the art is an act of illustration.

"Illustration assignments are not likely to provide a latitude for daring exploration or bold expression. So by most standards, the vast majority of renderings created to illustrate have no hope of succeeding as fine art," Selby opines. "This may well be the prime source of confusion and contention over the distinction between fine art and illustration.

"That said, there is a great wealth of wonderful work that begins—and ends—as illustration. We cannot conveniently dismiss out of hand all work that is commissioned to illustrate."

Book illustrations generally require three things: story, "page," and deadline. The story is text or words to illustrate. The "page" is the size, number, placement, etc., of the illustrations (as on the pages of a book). The deadline is when the work must be delivered.

Here (like Schmelzer), Selby also asks us to consider Michelangelo. "When Michelangelo was commissioned to paint the ceiling of the Sistine Chapel, he was given the story," he begins. "He certainly didn't write the Bible, and the text was not his personal expression.

"The ceiling of the Sistine Chapel replaced the pages of a book in a time of rampant illiteracy. In such a venue, throngs could view the finished ceiling all at once (as they have done for centuries now).

"Michelangelo set out to illustrate scriptures," says Selby understatedly. "Did his assignment to illustrate a book preclude the creation of a great work of art? I'll leave that to you."

Recently, art historians uncovered a vital communication from Michelangelo's rep to the artist prior to this very commission. Translated

© Bob Selby

from the Italian, the message reads: "Tell a complex story. Big job. Tough audience. Picky client. Screaming deadline. Money's not great. Interested?"

Does this sound vaguely familiar?

An American Illustration Timeline

The art of communicating through making marks is ancient and developing at light speed, as we speak. Prehistoric artists drew on cave walls. Now check out cuneiform and hieroglyphs. Study illuminated manuscripts. Look at engraving. Jump to lithography and photo-halftone, and then speed forward to the computer.

However, *American* illustration—obviously—is not too old. You might say it's in its early teen years. Let's take a beat (an admittedly *very* quick moment) to lightly appreciate the illustration family tree—your ongoing illustration experience blossoms directly from these roots.

1830s through 1900s. Currier and Ives, immensely popular nineteenth-century lithographers, fit the bill for superstar illustrators of their time. Their work truly characterizes that nostalgic era.

Winslow Homer epitomizes the war artist-reporters of the Civil War. Thomas Nast was the prototypical editorial illustrator of the mid-1800s. Likewise, counterparts like George Catlin, Frederic Remington, and Charles M. Russell documented American expansion west. Across the Atlantic, you'll find wonderful illustrators like Aubrey Beardsley in England and Gustave Doré in France.

In the **late 1800s**, you see "golden age" luminaries Charles Dana and Howard Pyle (often considered the father of American illustration).

1900–1920. The early twentieth century brings us color-halftone printing, plus illustrators like Jessie Willcox Smith, Violet Oakley, Joseph Clement Coll, the renowned N.C. Wyeth, Maxfield Parrish, and one of my personal all-time favorites, Franklin Booth.

1920–40. When discussing these years, two names may stand out: John Held, Jr., and Norman Rockwell. But also working now are illustrators like E. Simms Campbell (a pioneering illustrator of color), Maxfield Parrish, Rockwell Kent, John LaGatta, and Theodor Seuss Geisel (Dr. Seuss to us kids)!

A note about this era: The depression years of the 1930s may not offer a lot of happy stories. Like many folks of these tough times, some illustrators sold apples on the street and stood in soup lines. Busy, prolific illustrators in 1929 (it was not uncommon to make a *lot* of money in illustration, or to average a story a week) saw commissions plummet. Some illustrators were lucky to land a single assignment in the next years.

1940–1950. In the war years and after, we see master illustrators like Al Parker, Robert Fawcett, and Albert Dorne (founder-director of the Famous Artists School), plus another personal hero, Ben Shahn.

1950–60. Freelancers thrive. Conceptual illustration is a revolutionary direction of this era. Big budgets and big business. Big talent. Joe Bowler, Austin Briggs, and Al Hirschfeld are only a few of the great illustrators working here.

1960–present. Where to begin? I'll simply rattle off some names you just might recognize: Bernie Fuchs, Bart Forbes, and Mark English. Bob Peak. Milton Glaser, Saul Steinberg. Gary Kelley, C.F. Payne. Kinuko Craft. Anita Kunz. Gary Baseman.

The War between the States (of Mind)

Is illustration really art? Can illustrators call themselves artists? This great debate has been raging, well, since artists first called themselves illustrators. Illustrator Scott Bakal says it's certainly been a hot topic since the Abstract Expressionists came into being around World War II and the clash between the Abstractionists and the Representationalists of the time.

"In my opinion," he points out, "it doesn't matter. There is good art and bad art. Beyond that, it is just a never-ending fight over -isms and movements that will never really be won." Bakal continues: "Murray Tinkelman, a force in art and illustration for over fifty years, once commented to me that 'the difference between illustration and fine arts is that in illustration, the original is the reproduction.'

"This leads to the intent of use for the artwork created," Bakal elaborates. "The illustrator creates art for the specific purpose of getting the work published, where the fine artist generally does not.

"Humorously, I like Maxfield Parrish's comment on the difference between fine art and illustration: "The difference is about $30,000 a year.""

CHECKING IN

The preceding debate is merely an academic argument until you, the reader, buy into the myth of the so-called fine artist (or "illustrator"). What do these job titles mean to you? What do these labels really mean for *your* process and product?

In your heart of hearts, what are *you*? An illustrator, or a fine artist? There's really one true question: Does it matter to you—and why?

CHANGE OF (HE)ART

"My thinking has undergone a 360-degree spin in this area," illustrator Sarajo Frieden will tell you. "My suggestion is to *just get over it*. If you want to make art, make art. If you want to make illustrations, make them. Do both if it suits you. Make films and animations. Make toys and puppets; perform— if that's what *you* want to do. Get rid of rules, names, and anything that makes you smaller. Don't let anyone else define you."

Frieden's bilateral solution (aka good advice) is based on the wisdom of professional experience. "Illustration is kind of my latest career," she says. "I went to art school, waitressed, and then made my way up the food chain in the design world. Freelancing as a designer for the record industry somehow led me to more illustration and, voila, here I am, doing that artist/illustrator thing and everything else in between.

"I can't think of a time where this question has mattered less. The same inspirations that feed my personal/fine art work feed my commissioned work. I try to stretch and grow with *everything* I do. Hopefully that makes me more interesting and makes my work, whether for galleries or books or products, more interesting as well.

"I like to exhibit my personal work because it affords other unique opportunities, such as installation and seeing a body of work at one time. At the same time, I doubt that, even if it were possible, I would be interested in showing my work only in galleries, as if that were the *sine qua non* (the prerequisite) of visual hierarchy. I like that my illustration work is accessible and can be seen (and in some cases, used) by thousands or tens of thousands of people.

"We get caught in these dialogues about art/craft/illustration. Before there was 'art,' people were infusing utensils, cave walls, you name it, with embellishment and meaning. You walk into a store that sells beautifully designed products and you think, 'That vacuum cleaner is exceptional and will make cleaning more fun.'

"For the same reason, art is a usable commodity. 'I will put that painting up on my wall so that when I look at it, I am reminded that there is more to life than working or feeding the dog. That painting reminds me to dream.' At the end of the day, what is more useful?"

CHANGE OF MIND

"I used to believe any kind of commercial art was selling out," states illustrator Lauren Redniss. "I was sure I'd be a *painter*."

But after graduation, long days in an empty studio wore on her. "I was hungry to be learning more, to be more engaged in the world, to be working with interesting people." But unsure how to integrate these needs with her desire to be an "artist," Redniss explored other fields entirely.

She was employed at an art gallery (researching the dubious claims of a self-taught painter and inventor) and worked in a botanical lab documenting seed specimens. Redniss even rendered 300-million-year-old fossil turtles for the American Museum of Natural History. "I was agonizing over fractions of an inch," she recalls, "and my boss would still call the sketches 'loose.' I needed a middle ground between painting and scientific illustration."

So it was back to school. Redniss enrolled in the MFA program at the School of Visual Arts. "I didn't really know what illustration was beyond children's books. But it seemed to represent the chance to both write and draw, to collaborate with other people, to be surprised by those collaborations." It was also a sly subterfuge to create "art without worrying if it was important or new, or anything else that used to paralyze me when I picked up a paintbrush.

"I liked how accessible illustration was—how it was intended to be understood. This was more appealing to me than the gallery world, where work often seems deliberately obscure, or meant only for a rarefied audience."

The difference between an artist and an illustrator? "It doesn't make much difference to me," Redniss says. "I think an illustrator—someone who is commissioned to produce a visual representation for a specific purpose—can approach her work as art, and a so-called artist can produce paintings with no more soul than a bank logo.

"It is up to the individual to put herself into her work, to invest it with ideas and passion. This will come across in the final presentation, wherever it appears. Maybe that medium will be labeled 'illustration.' Maybe it will be labeled 'art,' or graffiti, or skywriting."

Redniss sums up by saying that it's all about the idea. "If you have concepts and you communicate them visually, you are an artist. If you can get those ideas into your commercial work, great. If they don't fit, find another medium."

CHANGE OF DIRECTION

Susan Guevara recently packed it up and relocated to a tiny town in northern New Mexico, about an hour's drive from both Taos and Santa

Fe. She found an old adobe with "two-foot-thick walls and old Saltillo floors. Enough room for *two* studios—one for book illustration, and another for painting."

In fact, that's exactly what she really came to do: paint. For some three years Guevara has quietly cultivated what she calls "a journey into my internal landscape." Dealing with a numbing creative block led her to Julia Cameron's book *The Artist's Way*. She also networked with other like-minded artists.

"It was clear I needed to better understand my own creative world, my own personal imagery, my own relationship to life (even the source of life and beauty, if I can be so unorthodox as to use those terms) through art."

Guevara learned a simple, joyful fact of life: "When something—music, visual, thought, folklore, philosophy, whatever—resonates within me, I had best pay attention." The visual "magical realism" she so aptly infused into her book *Chato and the Party Animals* took her search for resonance a step further.

Then she discovered "the most powerful taproot to the source I'd yet experienced. Mesoamerican imagery is a symphony to my internal imaginings. In indigenous thought and symbols I found a doorway into that private creative world that had been softly calling for a long time."

But Guevara also realized she needed to explore this connection without a due date or production restrictions, and particularly, without market limitations. A sluggish economy lent a hand. A lull in the market and tightening budgets slowed the industry down. A cherished book project was cancelled and is now in limbo.

But this economic downturn, along with other circumstances, led Guevara back to El Rito, New Mexico, where she had lived and painted seventeen years earlier. "The connection to this land and sky was powerful . . . all these years later I find myself here again.

"I'm still working on a couple of book projects, but my day starts with a cup of tea and an immediate walk across my dusty yard to the separate painting adobe.

"No phone comes with me, no music, even; only Nori, my newly rescued pound pup laying on the step." And Guevara walks with a renewed vigor, with "the complete self-acceptance and faith that led me through my first picture-book dummy, way back in the beginning of my career.

"In this studio I am starting that long journey an artist must inevitably make in order for her work to mature. At times I am scared. Mostly I am in awe and wholly thankful for the blessing of time—and for this big, big New Mexico sky."

CHANGE OF PLANS

Warren Chang was a professional freelance illustrator for twenty years, and from 1991 to 2001 alone, he painted close to 200 paperback illustrations for various publishers. He made a good living doing mostly commercial work for movies, advertising, and paperback books.

He modestly describes himself as a "journeyman" illustrator and comments that, "Aside from the Los Angeles Society of Illustrators, I was not recognized critically."

In 2001, Chang entered the world of fine art. Today, he makes his living primarily by selling his works in galleries and as a teacher of drawing and painting. But—and here it gets rather interesting—he continues to submit work to the Society of Illustrators "out of habit—although I do *very few* illustration jobs."

And ironically, since 2001, Chang has been repeatedly accepted into the annual society exhibitions (and *Communication Arts* illustration annuals). "Prior to 2001—as a full-time illustrator—my work was accepted only once by these institutions."

So go figure. And by that same token, Chang finds his illustration background greatly influencing his fine arts. "Although the fine art work is different from my previous illustration style," he comments, "it still maintains that somewhat narrative illustrative quality.

"During the time I worked as an illustrator, I thought I was doing something very artistic and creative. I was inspired by many of the great realistic illustrators and thought this was my opportunity to produce important work.

"It wasn't until I left the field that it became clear [to me] that my illustration work was too generic," he observes. But Chang acknowledges that much of what he learned as an illustrator has only helped his fine art career. (How to put a picture together and the importance of a strong work ethic are two such lessons.)

Chang recommends that an aspiring illustrator simply be a focused artist. "Try to become the best you can be," he will tell you. "Then use your skills and point of view toward whatever genre you choose, whether it be fine art or illustration. The best illustration transcends the field into fine art and vice versa."

TOUCHING BASE

The above stories are only interesting sidebars unless you, the reader, can check in with—and relate to—these issues along the way. So what about you? Our evolving life scenarios, changing plans (unexpected or otherwise), not to mention those little shifts in artistic temperament, are probably "business as usual" for all of us.

How do you handle your ebb and flow? Did a particular experience make you jump hoops or leap hurdles? Do you have what it takes to be an illustrator working with (or against) *your* odds?

Smile When You Say That, Partner

It's a safe bet that the tabloids would be out of business if celebrities weren't so quick to exhibit what is euphemistically labeled an "artistic temperament."

Illustrators may or may not be fodder for the gossip rags, but our ranks include the broad range of temperaments engendered by "the life." When you hear, "Well, what do you expect, she's an *artist*," it's usually accompanied by eyes rolling, a shake of the head, or a shrug of the shoulders. Don't forget that wry smile and knowing glance—the look that says "arty types" are just naturally "odd" or supposed to be "different."

For many of us, this is a bona fide rebel yell. Often we'll push the sharp edges and cultivate the differences just to spark that friction, regardless of the press we get. After all, a statement must be made (which is also part of the game).

FLAKES AND NUTS

This is nothing new. Choice tidbits about unpredictable behaviors and wild characters (plus the ever popular battle cry of "personal expression") have spiced up illustration history lectures ever since there was any history to address.

"I believe the idea of the 'temperamental artist' may have grown around the romanticism of van Gogh and his personal struggles—with a little Gauguin thrown in," muses illustrator Ray–Mel Cornelius. "No firm line here, but before Van Gogh, the artist was considered an *artisan*—a professional who worked within a framework of function, creating most of his work for the use or enjoyment of the Church or royal clients.

"Artists who had the inner drive to make beautiful images while working at the behest of such clients were unique individuals—it's not always an easy thing to pull off.

"Saying that, 'quirky' or 'flighty' could also act as a cover for a lack of professionalism. There is a difference in having an individual vision or unique point of view, and using that quality as an excuse or a euphemism for being a flake."

"There is an individualism necessary to develop your own style and become an illustrator," says PJ Loughran. "Because most illustrators work in seclusion, unaccountable to coworkers in their daily routine, some adolescent behavior may stick."

Asocial conduct—a surly disposition, lousy attitude, or inflated ego is tolerated (and frequently celebrated) in direct proportion to the success of the star. Our perception of who we're dealing with is only rivaled by our hero's self-perception.

It's a Small World after All

If we're trying to define what an illustrator is all about, we need to get personal right away—how do *you* define who *you* are? That answer differs with the individual, and your mileage may vary, but examine that issue first.

Now go a little bigger. How does the world define you? We can't poll every citizen of the planet, of course, so the more valid question might be: What is your *perception* of how the world sees you? This is where you'll probably operate from anyway. And a good, tough follow-up here is to consider the honesty of your answer. Can you separate self-perception from the real?

"My perception of how the world defines me is that I'm an illustrator first," comments illustrator Tuko Fujisaki. "In reality, this used to be very true, but I now have a much simpler life and different goals for myself."

Remember the slogan you saw on that VW minibus while mired in rush-hour traffic last week? "Think globally, act locally" wasn't phrased to address the field of illustration per se, but it resonates nicely for us. To me, that bumper sticker says we must effect change within the small space of who we are (and where) and then strive to expand that influence.

Sail On

If we are thinking globally, we must then ask: "Where is your place in the world?"

"I don't think a place in the world is something handed to me by virtue of my existence," illustrator Ilene Winn-Lederer says with splendid humility. "It appears that my assignment in this life is be an illustrator. It is up to me to create a niche with these skills to call my own, and work each day to maintain this position."

I think the above question is too big a chunk for most of us to bite off at one sitting. So let's practice some portion control: What is your place in *your* world?

Your world is as open-ended (or condensed) as you make it. So, when you think about your world, what are the boundaries—physical, mental, emotional, personal, and professional?

I'm sure there are folks who feel that their world is metaphorically flat, and that they will fall off the edge if they venture out too far. Life can be a dangerous place at times, and responsibilities are often scary destinations.

SALLY FORTH

So, if we share Winn-Lederer's mindset—that our assignment in this life is to be an illustrator—how are we handling the job? Some hypothetical answers to this question just might be:

1. I am efficiently using what I learned in art school and responding to my muse to live an active, creative life.

2. I am effectively utilizing my skills to support myself (and/or my family), and by fully tapping into my talents, I benefit those who need me the most.

3. I am speaking up with my creative voice to communicate to (or for) my community.

4. My art establishes who I am—as a unique person, as an individual artist.

These aren't the only answers, of course; it's your neighborhood, and we're only walking through it. I'm sure you've heard variations of this pep talk many times. But you know what? It's a good one, and it bears repeating.

Chutzpah and Humble Pie

A self-spoken, retiring demeanor isn't an illustrator's best approach if he wants to tackle the competition head-on and *stay* in business. There is a certain amount of necessary ambition involved in this business, and ambition often gets rather noisy.

By that token, bravado—true, honest daring—isn't necessarily a flaw in the diamond. "Some of this is actually a good thing," Loughran comments. "Self-confidence is a very important attribute to have as a self-employed person. Without it, an illustration *career* would be difficult, at best."

"I've always thought 'bravado' was usually the opposite side of 'insecurity,' at least in both of their excessive forms," adds Cornelius. "We all [as artists] have some of both. On the one hand, we think we have something worthwhile to say to the world. On the other, we feel we have *nothing* worthy to offer, and *we'll be found out* any minute.

"I guess that's where the ego steps in to provide enough confidence to move forward with the maturity to understand that there is a *balance*. I'm not sure what useful role fear might have (outside the obvious compulsion to keep a roof over our heads).

"Acceptance and rejection depend on that maturity to keep that balance between going forward and giving up. This maturity (understanding the realities of the world, *not* 'getting old' or losing a childlike sense of fun, experimentation, and wonder) may be the most useful attribute an artist can have.

"The healthy balance I refer to can help an art career, but I wouldn't say an art career 'nurtures' them. This healthy balance is the horse that pulls the career cart, not the other way around."

I HAVE MY DOUBTS ABOUT THAT

What about the other end of the straw: insecurity? Loughran approaches this issue from a great vantage point. "I think 'humility' is a better word for this," he says. "It's very necessary when seeking to make a living from your personal point of view."

And ego? "Everyone who seeks success in *any* field has a healthy sense of self," Loughran states. "Oftentimes, I think artists might be more susceptible toward that kind of criticism because the product we create is so closely tied to our personal perspective and 'who we are.' But in the end, confidence is essential in a field [like illustration] that depends so much on self-reliance."

Illustration as a Calling

Did you have some ardent urge to be an illustrator? Was there this gut feeling that art was what you *had* to do, that this line of work was *your* career path?

"I had no idea what illustration was," admits Bakal, "no concept of what it really meant to be an 'illustrator,' when I started. It actually had to be explained to me. I just considered myself an artist who liked the paintings that I saw in magazines and books.

"It worked for me. I have opinions and ideas. Illustration is a chance to get many of my ideas out there visually. Having the opportunity to visually expound on religion, politics, and social issues is stimulating and fresh.

"Keeping your vision of the world and how you present it in your illustration is the core of an illustrator's existence. If you can't hold onto that, then I feel you lose out on your own self-expression."

Your Mileage May Vary

In thinking about a creative life we all will face age-old quandaries concerning both the philosophy and the craft of art. These questions (and your particular answers) map the road trip of an illustrator's individual journey.

Before you meander that artistic path, understand that these questions are never really put to rest, but are frequently revisited and reevaluated as the artist/illustrator winds on down the road—as you've seen and will see throughout this book.

2

Art
Education

*From my first day in drawing class,
I knew I had found my niche. Art school
taught me how to see the world around me.*

—ERIN BRADY WORSHAM,
ILLUSTRATOR

Learning the Ropes   In this chapter we're going to talk about schooling, and the benefits of same. Even if you have talent, you still need practice to develop your chops. Ah, the formalities!

What's the most constructive way to gain that experience? Do you really *need* art *school*? That's a good question. Maybe not the toughest question on the art aptitude test, but definitely worth considering.

For my money, to compete in this field, some sort of art education is essential. You must learn the basics, understand the tools, and master the necessary skills to play the game well. Unless your name is Wyeth or Tintoretto,

© Tom Garrett

the best place I've found to do all this (in the shortest time possible, as painlessly as possible) is art school.

"It's true that some illustrators do not have formal training," says illustrator (and educator) Tom Garrett, "but I think that the majority of my students have gained a tremendous knowledge of the illustration field through a college program."

"I wouldn't be where I am today if it wasn't for my education at Parsons," illustrator PJ Loughran adds. "Art school gives you a chance to focus and develop the craft in a way that can't (usually) be done once you're out in the real world and financially independent."

Presenting an interesting (and objective) counterpoint, illustrator Alex Bostic picks up the thread. "Art education is never overrated," he says, "but in my experience—and maybe for better or worse—I've run into a lot of talented people who are very good, but never set foot inside an art building."

Here, Bostic pauses for a beat. "But there are certain things you must have to pull that off."

Like what? "You need to possess a natural curiosity and a lot of drive," Bostic continues. "Now a school situation always encourages drive," he points out.

"If you want to be in this field, you gotta have (or get) that motivation. It must become sort of embedded, ingrained—automatic. These 'self-schooled' individuals understand how to look at art, know to *study* art; they are *interested*, plain and simple. No one has to tell them to get up and paint that portrait in the morning. No one makes them keep a sketchbook."

And Ulana Zahajkewycz agrees. "Being self-taught still encompasses teaching," she says. "It involves that push and discipline, thirst for knowledge, and self-created structure. Few individuals have this sort of urge to succeed.

The Road Less Traveled

Hey, who's Les, and why didn't he go to art school? It is true—some artists don't go the "traditional" art education route. Brad Holland is probably my generation's classic example. You can mention R. Crumb (Robert Crumb) here, too.

However, life always offers educational alternatives (one way or another).

For instance, the largely self-taught (and Chicago-based) Holland served as an art assistant and apprentice (among other jobs). He eventually worked at Hallmark Cards (Kansas City, Missouri) prior to his arrival in New York City and becoming a force in the illustration world.

Crumb drew for American Greetings in Cleveland (and just about despised it), and worked as an assistant to the legendary Harvey Kurtzman—before San Francisco, *Cheap Thrills* (and LSD), and *Zap Comics*.

"That is not to say that you cannot find all of this on your own, in the out-side world—you most certainly can. Perhaps the school of life *can* be your instructor. It's up to the individual which path they take, to find the right fit for you."

Internships, Apprenticeships

Zahajkewycz mixed and matched her options to maximize her opportunities. While going for her MFA (in illustration) from the Minneapolis College of Art and Design, Zahajkewycz took advantage of the school's internship program.

Interns serve as apprentices under working professionals—it's a time-honored tradition. Often—and this will depend on the institution—it's without the structure of classes or the umbrella of the mothership. As an intern, you learn the foundations of business, mechanical skills, art history, and illustration fundamentals—all on a one-to-one basis.

Internships are just business as usual at better schools everywhere. As part of a school curriculum, these work situations aren't necessarily paying gigs, although outside of academia, an internship (or bona fide apprenticeship) may warrant compensation.

MENTORS

On the street, you may be working as an apprentice or intern, or you might just enjoy an official (or unofficial) mentor. A mentor is a guiding light, sometimes ceremonial, usually informal; it's a looser relationship with no paperwork involved and may have no strict workday or business hours (as there could be with an actual legal apprenticeship).

At school, a graduate program may function within that mentoring template. As Zahajkewycz tells us with considerable pride, "The mentored program at MCAD provided me with both the structure and the freedom I needed to create a new body of work, to really explore my style. This experience truly shaped my work into what it is today," she says.

Zahajkewycz also mentions illustrator Steven Guarnaccia as an important mentor. She worked in Guarnaccia's studio for roughly five years and found the experience absolutely invaluable.

"Seeing the day-to-day operations of an illustration business was an immeasurable help to me," she says. "Observing how an illustration veteran ran his shop is the type of experience I wish ALL illustration students

everywhere could get. Luckily, where I teach, there is an emphasis on intern-ships, so this is actually a reality for our students.

"The alternative to all this is to gain knowledge and skills through your own research (or by trial and error)," Zahajkewycz sums up.

Those choices work and are valid means to an end, of course—but why go it alone, if other opportunities are available to you?

Threading the Needle

A good art college offers a choice of degrees (a BFA and/or BA). There may be a graduate school (MA, MFA). The place might offer a continuing education program: night and/or weekend classes, and these days, maybe the option to get a degree online.

You'll see a range of related creative programs: illustration, design, fine arts, comic art, anime/manga, sculpture, 3-D, animation, interactive media, etc.

Within this cornucopia of disciplines you'll find the Foundations and Intro courses, standard fare like Figure Drawing and Painting sections, as well as sister classes (a Type and Image class, for instance)—all designed to sharpen your mechanical chops (through both traditional and digital media), compositional skills, and color sense.

Here you will take courses that make you *think* as well as *do*: those all-important conceptual, communication, and problem-solving skills. Beyond the courses in general (and specific) techniques, you'll get some art theory/phi-losophy and history (you could major in these as well).

Many institutions will send you out on an internship (an apprenticeship) for one or two semesters. Maybe there will be a chance to do a semester (or year) abroad at a sister school. There's often a directed seasonal tour or class abroad as well.

Better schools offer classes in the *business* of illustration as well as marketing and promotion. There should be intensive professional practices and portfolio development (at least one course, and usually in the last semester of your senior year).

As a coda here I want to stress the significance of your business education. Because after school (and after all), you will be *in business*. "Back in my school days," illustrator Rick Tulka says, "there's one thing I never got at Pratt in the illustration department. In fact, I never learned it in any classes.

"I don't know if they are teaching this now, but I feel every illustration student should have a class in the business of illustration." (Author's Note: They do, indeed. It's called "Freelancing and Business," and it covers Tulka's wish list below—and more).

"What I would've given to know so much of what I learned the hard way," Tulka sighs. "For example: pricing and billing, contracts and payment, copyrights, job-search strategy and portfolio prep, making contacts, interview/résumé skills, plus small-business info—taxes, deductions, contracts and copyrights, work for hire, etc. That was all picked up as I did it, on the job."

© Rick Tulka

TULKA

Check out *your* prospective alma mater. Make sure you will get a business education as part of the deal. And then pay attention.

Big Wheels

What are the skill sets an illustrator should take away from school? Listen to me carefully here: If you don't know how to draw, if you don't live for (and love) illustration, I wouldn't go to art school to become an *illustrator*.

An illustration department is *not* the place to *learn how to draw*. It is a place to learn how to draw *better*, to maximize your natural (but existing) drawing chops, to intensively and extensively explore the craft and concept (the who, what, when, why, and, yes, how) of drawing.

Drawing is the core of all creative endeavors. Strong drawing skills are a plus in any artistic discipline. But if your drawing acumen is weak, or you really don't know what else to do creatively (or illustration "sorta interests me, and my guidance counselor said I should go to art school"), I'd think again about studying to "become an illustrator." I like to play Yahtzee, but it would've been a mistake for me to major in math.

Saying that, there *are* illustrators who display what is euphemistically called a "minimal" drawing style. How do they survive in a world of incredibly sharp pencils (and sharper pencil jockeys)? More often then not, it's because their *conceptual skills* are that good. No, "good" isn't strong enough; their ideas are world-class—the other important piece of the puzzle being that these minimalists have enough mechanical ability to sell those concepts visually.

I won't get into the debate of what's *more* important, conceptual or mechanical skills (at least for now). We can make the argument for one, the other, or both in combination. But the question was: What are the skill sets an illustrator should take away from school?

It's simple: Roll out of school with mechanical skills *and* conceptual skills (and if one of those wheels is flat—or missing—the presence to know how to ride a unicycle).

Two-Year or Four-Year

So you've decided to go to art school. Good call. But choosing a school is a complex and important decision. Is a two-year school better than a four-year art program? And what are some of the factors a potential student should look at when picking out a school?

The answer can depend on your needs and attitudes, as well as your personal goals and timetable.

Tom Garrett is design chair at the Minneapolis College of Art and Design. As both a seasoned professional and a master teacher, he has pertinent comments when asked to discuss the art education of illustration students. "I believe the difference between a four-year program versus two-year vocational training is that the emphasis is placed on learning new ways of problem solving," he says.

"In a rigorous four-year program the student gains a whole range of skills. Students have the time to grow and develop multiple professional solutions to one assignment.

> *Some see illustrators as privileged individuals who screw around and get paid for it. Many nonartists have no appreciation for the years of learning that go into even the most basic of art making.*
>
> *Granted, there are those who seem to spring fully formed from the womb, creating incredibly inventive work—but these illustrators are few and far between.*
>
> —KEN MEYER, JR., ILLUSTRATOR

"Along with making images, students learn how to verbally communicate their ideas and gain an understanding of the professional world with exposure to the best business practices and ethics.

"Finally, a longer program enables the student to be aware of the history of illustration and its context with other disciplines, like graphic design, fine arts, fashion, and architecture. The outcome often means that the student is not just mimicking the latest styles. Instead, he is learning ways of being more innovative. This approach also prepares the student for changes in the field down the road (in regard to technology, the economy, and artistic growth)."

These Dreams

Illustrator Ken Meyer, Jr., admits to a mistake. "I wasted my first college days," he says candidly, "basically just played and slept—and I feel I have developed 'holes' in my knowledge."

But Meyer decided to meet the problem head-on; *he went back to school.* "I am learning many things I wasn't able to articulate, basics I can now apply that I didn't pick up on my own. Plus, being around other students is an eye-opening learning experience in itself—even for me, an illustrator who has worked some twenty years."

How does the aspiring illustrator looking to go to college check his wishes and his goals against the practical issues of the real world? If you are considering art school, here's a quick personal checklist and minitest to start off.

1. First ask yourself what you're ultimately getting out of art school. What's on the next page when you book out of college? So, why bother . . . what will you personally and professionally gain? Answer honestly. A good-paying job? That prestigious career? The jump start to a life-long learning opportunity? You just want to meet chicks or a nice guy?

2. Do you have the drive and ambition to make this next two to four years of your life a positive, productive experience? And in those two to four years, can you hone the skills that will bring you success after art school? And remember: Talent without drive and motivation does not generate income.

3. Away from school, it's not such a controlled experiment. Are you self-disciplined? Are you decisive? If you don't learn this at school, when? Student drudgeries (and commitments) usually pale in comparison to what you'll deal with as a real working stiff. At school (as in the "real world"), a poor attitude will cripple your workday, and lackadaisical habits will get you into trouble very quickly.

4. Can you thrive on competition? By and large, I'm sure your art school days will be some of the best (and most fun) years you'll ever have, but better schools are tough microcosms of the illustration biz— boot-camp training grounds for the studio life.

5. How do you handle stress? The considerable tensions of academia will give you a chance to meet some old clichés head-on—all that grace-under-pressure, rolling-with-the-punches, and thinking-on-your-feet stuff.

The Gig from There

Many elements factor into a "successful" career. Sure, there's luck involved—I wouldn't curse good fortune (especially as it translates into job opportunities). Location may enter into the equation—where you do business can be a factor, not to mention being in the right place at the right time (more luck).

Attitude—either positive or negative—may be part of the mix. Who you know can make a difference. Perseverance comes into play. Energy and stamina are crucial in both the long and short terms. If you are into sales (you are selling your illustration, are you not?), business acumen just makes simple sense.

And then there's a little thing called aptitude. Talent—the natural ability to do something well—must be a prerequisite. Are there individuals who make it with nominal gifts? Without a doubt, and you'll find them in every endeavor. But if quality is critical, I'll go with chops and panache every time.

Well, Do I Really Need Continued Education?

Learning is a life-long process. Life is nothing but a learning curve. Your education should never cease. For many illustrators, the undergraduate degree is just the first stop.

There are those graduates who hit the ground running right out of college. Here, the realities of maintaining a career (and running a business) define the word "school" in the purest sense of the term. Or you may find an apprenticeship. This is not as common a work relationship as it once was in the "old days," but I hear about modern apprenticeships all the time (see chapter 2).

MAKE THE GRAD

But loads of artists looking to take their game to a higher plateau go for a graduate degree as the next best step.

As previously mentioned, MCAD offers a mentor-based graduate program that (in their words), "combines the freedom of open studio work with structured feedback, critiques from visiting artists, and liberal arts seminars . . . an enriched, intense, and interdisciplinary experience."

"Education as an artist is so important," says illustrator Scott Bakal, picking up this thread. "Some people disagree, but I feel being in a learning environment with your peers and learning new classic and contemporary illustrators, techniques, and styles will only help your grow as an artist.

"Even if this doesn't improve your style, you'll gain that knowledge (which is just as important). Knowing what is happening around you in the field and what has happened in the past will help you make better decisions as your career progresses forward."

This is not just idle chatter for Bakal. In 2004, after eleven years illustrating, he decided to apply to a master's in illustration program. "I felt I needed a psychic and creative kick in the ass," he confesses. "I put myself around other creatives and working illustrators to feel that competition and get that sense of group self-exploration again. I wanted to explore new ideas and see how others in the industry are operating.

"You need not be going back for another degree. I would, however, always recommend a continuing education class—at the very least, a drawing class where you are surrounded by other artists.

"Watching my classmates and seeing how they went from their roughs to comps to finished product was such a learning experience. It has opened new doors in how I develop an illustration."

SUMMER CAMP

Do investigate summer workshops like the Illustration Academy. At these programs, the industry's biggest and brightest creatives share both technical prowess and business savvy via intensive, real-world assignments (including the prerequisite screaming deadlines).

The workload is great, the critiques are tough but honest, and the hands-on demos alone are worth the cost of tuition. Both current students (as well as their teachers) and seasoned pros take advantage of these wonderful learning opportunities—and so can you!

GO WEST OR HEAD EAST

Travel can certainly expand your education. "Travel" as a learning experience—even if you cannot leave the country—expands your horizons, clears the head, and opens your eyes. Isn't this what any good education should do?

"Being curious and open to change keeps me moving and fuels my work," Garrett states enthusiastically. "In the summertime, when I'm not teaching, I try to jump on a plane and see some new place or experience some new thing. I recently traveled to Buenos Aires. Two years ago, I spent some time in Saigon. I came back from both trips charged with new ideas and, in the case of Vietnam, a new love of color."

It's truly a world community for Jenny Kostecki-Shaw, who's a veteran globe hopper. "Travel opens me," she tells you. "For me, it is about letting go of judgments and expectations; being open to different things and all they have to teach me."

BE A SPONGE: LEARNING FROM FELLOW PRACTITIONERS

"Art school, for me, was just great," Lori Osiecki will tell you. "It gave me the opportunity to experiment with different media, connect with other creative people, and learn how to pull it all together so that I could actually support myself doing something I enjoy. It doesn't get any better than that."

But during her last months at school, Osiecki utilized her student status to earn some practical, real-world credits. She wrote to all the design firms in her area—advertising agencies, magazines, any art director who would be willing to spend fifteen minutes with the budding illustrator. She scheduled meets whenever she was free (usually Fridays).

These weren't interviews, per se. Osiecki was networking—a time-honored method to establish business contacts, enhance your education—even make new friends. So she made it clear she was *not* asking for work, just some *advice*.

"I really valued what they had to offer in terms of direction, criticism—anything," she tells you. "I wanted to shape my portfolio. I wanted to be able to find a job. I did not want to do something else to support my art habit."

Osiecki found that her contacts were incredibly generous with their time. And she listened to what these art directors had to say, reworking her book so that *she* felt good about her work. As a direct result, she conquered certain fears, and became less nervous about the interview process.

"And, luckily for me," she says, "I landed my first job within two months of graduating. It was a fine job and a wonderful experience—I worked for Hallmark Cards, where I had the good fortune of meeting and working with some of the best artists in the country.

"I left Hallmark in the late eighties, but I still keep in touch with many of the people I met. Creative bonding—there's nothing like it!"

Training and Discipline

What are the skill sets one needs to be an illustrator? Discipline is indeed one of the qualities you need to develop to have a successful career. Can you learn this? Is this part of an illustrator's education?

Sure. I believe you can train (and educate yourself) to either accept or develop discipline (and perhaps you need both). Perfecting this particular skill set is often motivated by a heavy workload or precipitated by a missed deadline. And yes, the school of hard knocks always offers night courses.

There's a lot to be said for such on-the-job training. For many illustrators, the combination of drive, hard work, and basic chops is the best art school (even *after* two to four years of actual art school).

©LoriOsiecki

© Lori Osiecki

"I look back at myself and think I was a pretty strong art student," says illustrator Doug Klauba. "But by the time I got out of school, I realized I had *so much more* to learn and I needed a little further direction. But I also saw that I really needed to take this direction from *myself*."

Of course, you have to be able to *draw* and *think*. "Drawing skills and concepting are key," asserts illustrator Benton Mahan. "You must be able to think things through *and* express those ideas visually. If you can't do this, then you've failed.

"Your work ethic—your focus—is vital," he continues. "You improve, get better. *Motivation* is more important than talent. If you are motivated, you will figure out what you can do with the talent you have."

Before I went to art school, I pooh-poohed the idea of going to art school. I was convinced I knew everything I needed to know. The truth was that I was afraid—afraid I might discover I had no talent.

But now I was thinking in terms of color, design, and technique. It didn't affect my imagination; it just gave me the tools to bring my ideas to fruition.

—ERIN BRADY WORSHAM, ILLUSTRATOR

"And then it's all about your track record," adds Alex Bostic. "What you are capable of doing, the reputation you build, how credible you are. Credibility is so important, and credibility is established by making deadlines.

"To me, reliability is more important than skills. Skill and talent run a close second. Sure, you must be good, but you have to be reliable. I've seen people who are not particularly skilled, but still get a lot of work. Why? Because they are reliable.

"If you're a talented guy and you don't come through, all the talent in the world is *not* going to get you more jobs," Bostic cautions. "If you're talented *and* reliable—that's great. Talent rules. But reliability is king.

"Miss a deadline and that can be the kiss of death for your career. Nobody wants to hear your personal problems when it comes to their project. They want to know, *Is it done or not?* And you are in the business to get the job done."

Life's Lessons

Maybe your circumstances are such that you cannot go to art school. Perhaps you already have a non-art job and you cannot afford to leave it. This is not an insurmountable obstacle.

© Jenny Kostecki-Shaw

As Kostecki–Shaw comments, "Life experience also offers a good art education. Ben Shahn advised us to not disregard anything. If you can't go to school or can 'only' get a job in an auto factory, then do that. If your head and heart are open to all possibilities, it's not 'just work.' Observe, feel, touch, believe, and think—all this can come out in your art.

"Shahn just drew and drew all the time. If you constantly want to draw and create and you think about only that, you're an artist—it's actually that simple."

STIMULATIONS

Kostecki–Shaw's comments are well grounded. Life lessons learned can certainly be practical fodder for your art.

Hello, fodder? Yes—the *Encarta World English Dictionary* definition for this term is a perfect match for our concept here: "people, ideas, or images that are useful in stimulating a creative or critical response."

Ever since I was a kid I loved making things. My mother encour-aged me in all creative pursuits. I'm sure that this early working with many different kinds of materials helped to form my love of mixed media.

—SUSAN FARRINGTON, ILLUSTRATOR

Ben Shahn was a social realist: His work was often inspired by the news, and he literally drew from events that impacted his world around him.

One extension of this direction would be environmental structures like the remarkable Watts Towers in Los Angeles. A "common worker," Simon Rodia, raised the sculptures using basic tools and recycling throwaway materials (glass, shells, pottery, tiles, and mortar).

Rodia worked more than thirty years (1921 to 1955) on his homage to America—it's a tribute to the creative spirit and the dream of a better life. If that's not what art is all about, I'm not sure what is.

Another resonant case in point would be Harvey Pekar, whose autobiographical comic book series *American Splendor* (sparked by collaborations with A-list illustrators like Robert Crumb) led to television appearances, awards, and a later movie.

The School Bell

"There are many valid styles of learning," comments Tom Garrett. How true. Learning is synonymous with growth and development—extended avenues of thought or action. Art education is a life-long endeavor. This real-world training never stops. We're "at school" every day.

We're always acquiring knowledge, and it's truly a two-way street. Within the circle of your world, you live, you learn, you teach daily—one on one. As illustrators, we have a really nice gig—maybe we have something we want (or need) to say. Our illustration can get that message out to a wide audience. Maybe someone, somewhere, can learn something via our communication skills. And, even sweeter, perhaps we can put bread on the table doing it.

It's school with an "open door" policy—a wonderful open house of creative stuff.

3
Mechanical Skills

In terms of expressing the human condition,
technology has always been the means,
art the ends.

—BRAD REED, DESIGNER
  AND EDUCATOR

Talent and Tech   Why is it important to discuss technical skills? This chapter will offer an evaluation of the technical skills aspiring illustrators will need, and how far (and where) those technical skills may take you. We'll examine other talents you will need, and how technology has impacted the illustrator's necessary skill set. We'll also offer some suggestions on how to upgrade your technical tool kit.

The Means, Not the End

Illustrator Benton Mahan calls himself "old school." "We just did things," he says, smiling, "and didn't 'think it through' so much." A seasoned veteran,

Mahan isn't slamming his generation of illustrators at all. He's only saying his peers did the job intuitively. "Illustrators these days are more attuned to a *process* you go through," he says.

What does Mahan mean by this? Let me reiterate something he says in chapter 2: What's important to the modern illustrator's process? Drawing. Concepting. Thinking things through. Research. Great concepts; the ability to express those ideas visually. Your work ethic—focus, *hard work*. Improving; getting better. *Motivation.*

"One current trend I notice is that the process has become more group oriented," Mahan points out. "Maybe that's because of the variety of students coming up. Folks these days are very willing to work as part of a team (as part of a crew of animators, for instance). I think the computer (and working dig-itally) plays a big part in this."

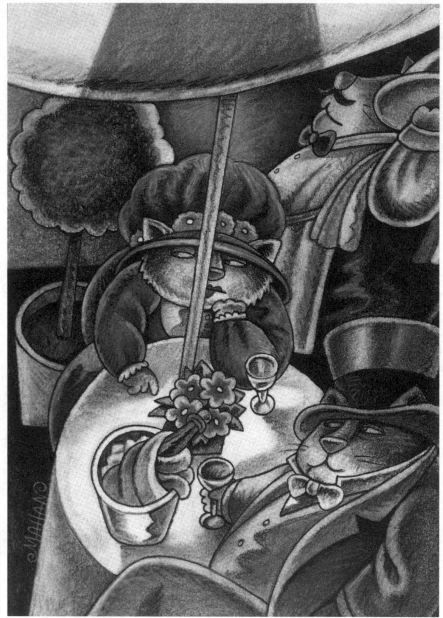

48   HOW TO GROW AS AN ILLUSTRATOR

Tech It to the Limit

As illustrator Darren Booth points out, "Technology has been a major contributor to the development of contemporary illustration, so staying current with technology is extremely important to illustrators."

You don't need to be the fastest chip on the motherboard to see that he's right, of course. From the actual look of the art (creation and production) to the back end, technology impacts the process.

LEADING THE CHARGE

This is nothing really new. There have been many sea changes throughout illustration history. One might argue that the digital age is perhaps a *tsunami* of change, but that's not the point of the discussion here.

Technology has always been an evolutionary, if not revolutionary, fact of life for illustrators. One case in point: For most of the nineteenth century, there were not many venues for American illustration, or any pressing need for art, beyond the regional or personal level. But the Civil War—and steady advances in printing technology, supplies, and materials—created new markets and spawned a burgeoning field: the illustrated weekly and monthly magazines. The public demanded news—and pictures. Thus was born the epoch of the field reporter (aka artist-reporter).

You may have heard of Currier and Ives (and their kindred competitors). These immensely popular nineteenth-century lithographers depicted breaking news events (or simply celebrated daily life). Done in litho—a new process in the 1800s—such work could be turned around quickly and efficiently. The reproductions were sold on street corners in incredible numbers.

With fame and financial success came the means to hire better artists and feed *better art* to an enormous, hungry market.

We take the old technologies for granted and forget that they were once new.

—DARREN BOOTH, ILLUSTRATOR

As visuals were incised into wood blocks or metal plates, this was "what–you–see–is–what–you–get" technology in a primitive form. But if an artist lacked those skills, an intermediary—the engraver—redrew the picture to the plate or block.

The relationship between the artist and the engraver was always a bit of a balancing act. As printing technology developed—the lithography process, engraving techniques—larger print runs plus better reproduction was a result.

Then, at the turn of the nineteenth century, came the extraordinary breakthrough of the photo–halftone process. Developed at the end of the 1800s, this photo–mechanical method combined photography and halftone engraving. Better and faster printing presses, a growing audience with a huge appetite for product, plus photo–halftone triggered the hallowed "golden age of illustration."

THE MORE THINGS CHANGE

This scenario should sound familiar to you. Yes, the computer has indeed changed "everything" over our last two decades. "Yo, man—it's *all* different," you say. But if you study illustration history, you'll see this "brave new world" cliché is *business as usual* with every generation of illustrators, in any period, for all genres.

Any technical (plus social and cultural) revolution has impacted the skills needed by then–modern illustrators. Color–halftone printing revolutionized the industry in the early twentieth century. Big budgets (and big business) of the 1950s meant freelancers (and big art studios) could thrive.

© Julia Minamata

Also in this period came a newfangled must-have. The television drew advertising dollars away from the magazines and challenged illustrators to tell a story in a different (i.e., more riveting) manner.

Illustrators rose to the occasion. Conceptual illustration became the revolutionary direction, as artists mined diverse materials to explore abstract and representational expressionism. Now, modern—as well as primitive and comic—art became an accepted reference. Illustrators boldly played with the very metaphor and symbolism rejected by a previous creative generation.

As illustrator and educator Tom Graham points out, "The field *is* different. Since I've been teaching the history of illustration for the past few years (and learning it myself), I realize it has always changed, sometimes radically. But it's maybe the best time to be young and an artist!"

But there's only the here and now for you—this is *your* best time to be an illustrator. And like Howard Pyle, who was *all over* half-tone reproduction and took that then-new technology to greater heights, you're going to make the most of *our* brave new world.

The Joy of Tech

"Is art created with a paintbrush better than art created by a software program?" asks illustrator Scott Bakal. Good question. Does the medium affect the message? "It perplexes me why so many artists are still so adamant about using traditional materials," he continues. "Working with software programs such as Photoshop or Painter is just like working with a more traditional tool such as a sable or bristle brush—with a few aesthetic and editing differences."

What divides people in this sometimes heated debate? Working in the field while teaching both digital and traditional illustration has taught Bakal that the computer makes it possible for artists of all stripes to create "good" *and* "bad" art.

"A person unable to convey the basics of art and design won't be able to produce better art simply by virtue of employing this complex and modern tool," Bakal reasons. "This person may believe he can fake original illustration, but savvy viewers easily recognize the plethora of standard Photoshop filter effects."

© Scott Bakal

Bakal is saying that the computer can't take the place of traditional tools or standard hand skills. "If you believe so, you're sorely mistaken," he cautions. "Someone using the computer as a tool to create art needs to be educated in the basic foundations of drawing practice and theory.

"At school, I was told time and time again that before an artist is able to create a good painting, he needs to be able to create a good drawing. I feel that this still holds true, even (and especially) in the digital age."

GIFTED

If this particular discussion of "good "versus "bad" art feels like just one small part of the debate, you're right. So, for instance, what about a learning curve?

Well, the learning curve to make bad or good art is all relative. A year is a year on every calendar. Practice won't make perfect, and to get anywhere, you must perform. What's the cliché: Life is not a rehearsal? Trite, but right. This old saw works for art, too.

We all have our gifts. There's a big difference between perception and perspiration. However, one guy can invest considerable time and energy and never quite "get the hang of it," while another displays a considerable knack after a brief glance at the specs (or minor practice). We're not punching the art clock . . . put in your eight-hour day and another Mona Lisa pops off the creative assembly line.

CAN YOU TOP THIS?

Who is to say my hand skills are better than yours? You might. And I might, too. I can do many things with a pen and a brush. I have certain talents—but I can never do what you do. And besides, I don't want to—I think that's the sane perspective. Now, if you're my surgeon and we're at opposite ends of my appendectomy, we hopefully won't enter into this debate at all.

And what about people who prefer to create only where there is a tactile element involved? This is kind of a nonargument to me. If it doesn't hurt anyone, and it brings you joy, just go ahead and create in your manner.

"Everything you touch comes via your intuition," Paul Melia says. "And when you pull things out, it should all come together in some way to bring out your own style. It should give you a wonderful sense of accomplishment to do something unique, and that will come from every direction you can find."

DO IT YOURSELF

What is involved in translating drawing skills, assuming you already possess them, to the computer? Not much! The computer should simply be another tool in your art box. I love to paint with inks and acrylics—*and* Photoshop. To me, either/or is purely a matter of choice and purpose.

It's not the brush that lays down a juicy watercolor wash; it's your skill in manipulating that media. It's not your Mac that really makes that buttery gradation in Corel Painter. *You* make it happen.

So, just as you learn how to manipulate that sable brush to get a certain watercolor effect, you learn how to control a computer (and tools) to keep that thread going.

SHHH . . . IT HAPPENS

We can't blame "bad" art solely on the rise of the computer, although many folks are prone to do just that. As Bakal points out, "Bad art happens—

it hangs in galleries throughout the world, and is found widespread in print." It could simply mean an inept artist or faulty art direction; both bad art and good art exist, regardless of medium.

Bakal notes cultural and societal aspects to this discussion as well. "If we look back to 1995 we can recognize that over the past decade or so, there've been enormous shifts in computer usage within the illustration industry. Indeed, in how society—and clients—view and purchase art and illustration, as well," he says. (Reader: Please refer to our continued discussion of changes in the industry in subsequent chapters.)

ONE-ROOM TOOLBOX

Mahan says he's also aware of how industry trends make an impact on an academic level. "The curriculum is shifting," he explains. "Media studies— video games, entertainment, etc.—are on the rise. For a lot of students, that's their thing, what they're going into. So traditional *skills*—drawing and color theory, let's say—are not a primary focus for students.

"The ideal scenario would be to have the drawing foundation built into the technical program—all artists need the drawing skills. Companies hire based on drawing skills *and* technical savvy. These days, it's almost taken for granted that folks understand the basic hardware and software, but good modelers, sketch artists, or designers are a little harder to find."

> *[You can take] a very journalistic approach. I'm a very visual person. I learn by seeing. Even the way I learned to read and write: I learned by drawing out the letters, and rewriting the letters. If you're defining drawing as making marks on a page, then definitely, it's about learning.*
>
> —MARCOS CHIN, ILLUSTRATOR

And Bakal agrees. "My twenty-first-century classes have no real idea about how the industry worked just ten years ago. When I show them a mechanical and some shoddy press type and explain the process of creating art prior to 1990, I usually get a giggle or two and a certain amount of disbelief.

"Every year, every semester, more and more students eschew the paintbrush and prefer to work digitally. In their 'modern' world, it makes sense to them; they do not need a physical original to get their creative points across. They just want to create the best art they can with the technology readily available."

In my discussions with Bakal and other illustration educators, I hear that same refrain: Students in older age brackets may still prefer to work traditionally, but digital methods are preferred by the new generations of artists. "The trend shows no sign of reversing," Bakal tells us, "and this slow yet visible shift is creeping into the buyer mindset as well. Art directors (and general art buyers alike) are viewing a creative image—digital or traditional—on its own merit.

FOR WHOM THE DELL TOLLS

If you factor in the speed, efficiency, and convenience of marketing, producing, and delivering digital illustration, does this shift mean the eventual death of handmade art? I say not. Bakal is one artist who skips back and forth between traditional and digital media. And look at the work of Chris Spollen (and others).

I jump this fence as well. Like Bakal, I enjoy both worlds. For instance, using programs like Corel Painter, ArtRage, Studio Artist, and the queen of the prom, Adobe Photoshop, you can easily recreate the coloring, structure, blending, and even the textural look of a traditional painting. "The final printed product means the viewer won't be able to physically see the bumps and ridges of the paint on the canvas," Bakal points out. "The eyes are fooled into thinking this surface actually exists, but it doesn't. However, there is no way to tell if it was produced traditionally or digitally."

It's an uneducated view that creating digital work is easier, simpler, and/or faster to create than traditional art. If you think this way, I'd venture to say you really haven't actually illustrated on the computer.

"Digital illustrators," as Bakal sums up, "know that this is far from the truth. You still need to know how to draw and blend color, color theory, working with tone—all the standard rules apply. It's simply created on a screen rather than on paper or canvas."

Better Business by Bits and Bytes

If you currently work as an illustrator but have fallen a bit behind the technology curve, this might be a good time to reevaluate the advantages of staying on the cutting edge. Take Darren Booth, for example.

Although his work is traditionally executed, Booth makes it a point to keep up with technology. From marketing and promotion to production, preparation (color correction, etc.), and delivery, technology streamlines Darren's time and makes his art director's life easier.

"Technical expertise fosters good business skills as well—making the process as easy and fluid as possible always helps ensure more work.

"In a way, I *try* to cater to people's laziness," he says. "For example, e-mailing is a great way to send a job, but sometimes presents file-size limitations. I deliver my work simply by uploading it to my Web server, then send the corresponding Web link to the AD. The AD clicks on the link and it downloads right to her desktop.

"Digital delivery also means I can keep the original art in my studio, where I don't have to worry about shipping (which means time and money). I don't have to sweat the piece getting damaged or lost."

In some cases, Booth even bills the client for scanning. He has found this to be a touchy subject for some of his fellows, but for Booth it's just a pure (and smart) business decision. "When I scan, prep, and digitally deliver the art, I'm saving the AD (and her organization) time and money. My fees are almost always lower than the potential shipping cost.

© Darren Booth

"I'm up front with my charges, and the small costs usually depend on final size and scale, so if it takes me a long time to scan and prep, I charge them. If it's an easy scan and prep, no charge."

Love It All

How should the reader approach technology? In our day and age, you can still be a "traditional illustrator" with a vengeance. The techniques and hand skills that have always driven illustration (and fine arts) are alive and well.

Some of us demonize "computer art." This could be a backlash towards a perceived automation of the artistic process. Perhaps we fear the watering down of hand skills. Maybe we don't want to cater to the undo demands of a fickle, impatient customer base (and a short product shelf-life)? And we can't deny simple, good sense—"If it ain't broke, don't fix it." But it doesn't matter. There is room in that artbox for both old and new toys.

I doubt that any schools are teaching a Drawing 101 class on computers—that's going about the task back-asswords. The fundamentals have been a constant for centuries—foundations are laid by hand with traditional utensils. You then progress to doing handwork with the power tools.

I've also heard the rumblings that it will be a "paperless" world for years now. I won't predict the future, but it hasn't happened, and I'm betting (and hoping) it doesn't go down that way.

I *love* working on the computer. But hand rendering on a tactile surface, physically holding the piece to the light, seeing art in real dimensions, is just amazing—simply soul-satisfying.

But you know, if I juggle some of those words around, I feel the same way about working digitally. What can I say? I just love doing art in all its manifestations, with *all* the apparatus.

BRAVE? NEW WORLD?

Why wait to jump on the bandwagon? Why take partial steps? Why be a technophobe? How will any of that benefit you in this global community today?

If you don't want to create on the computer, don't—it's that simple. However, if you're interested in timely (and efficient) modern communications, plus current business and delivery systems, I don't see how you can, would, or should avoid the computer—it's that simple.

4
Conceptual Skills

Personal preference notwithstanding,
the quality of art is not about which tool
is better than another—it is about the
art and the artist.

—SCOTT BAKAL, ILLUSTRATOR

Concept: What an Idea!   Is it obvious that in addition to mechanical aptitude, an illustrator needs strong ideas? Why is it advantageous for illustrators to grow in this arena?

A flair for the conceptual is a particularly enriching option in the illustrator's tool kit. Let's take some time to think out and answer a few questions about the matter of conceptual skills.

Perception

People perceive—observe and identify—in many different ways. Our sense of perception is affected by a number of factors, including location, lifestyle, the nature/nurture thing, and, of course, personal taste.

© Gregory Nemec

We also visualize—we dream and imagine: We "see it in our mind's eye." One asks, "Can you picture it?" You just might declare, "I have a vision." So, keep it in mind.

There's "looking" and "seeing," and the trick is to form that image—visualize—and take it all in. "*Look.* Can you *see* it?" Illustrator Gregory Nemec says it well: "You must use your eyes, then comprehend."

It's akin to the relationship between "hearing" and "listening." *Hearing* is passive . . . "I *hear* voices somewhere." *Listening* is active . . . "Shhhh . . . let me *listen* to this song on my iPod."

What Are Conceptual Skills?

Illustrations are certainly *looked at* in the physical but perhaps *seen* in an intellectual sense. I'm fudging here, but with a smile. You might *see* this state-ment, and maybe *look at* it another way.

On the surface, how we direct eye movement is essential to what illustration is all about (and by direct relation, what composition is all about).

Conceptual skills are thinking skills. "More specifically," as illustrator Tom Garrett says, "conceptual skills are communication skills. As in: How do we as illustrators communicate difficult and complex ideas in a picture?"

> *Here's the question: How does one discern the sublime from the ordinary? One makes a judgment based on experience, instinct, and knowledge. Like love or truth or any other quality that evades easy definition, you will know it when you see it.*
>
> —PAUL DALLAS, ILLUSTRATOR

Illustrators have always told stories in their images (think Norman Rockwell). However, in the last decades, many illustrators have been asked to go beyond obvious narrative—telling a story—and develop the content of their ideas with metaphors and symbols.

For instance, your assignment (for *Time* magazine) is to draw the nasty leader of a Third-World nation known for its wanton expansionism. The unthinkable has just happened: This oppressive regime has tested a nuclear device. In your illustration, you depict the evil dictator as a monstrous vampire posed over the exposed neck of a helpless woman. Her draping garments are actually the flags of the offender's neighboring nations; his fangs are decidedly bomb shaped.

HIGH CONCEPT

"The ability to formulate an image that can address an assignment in a unique, original way," says illustrator Ilene Winn-Lederer, "is considered *high-concept* illustration. It marries your own life experience to historic/contemporary precedents."

What Winn–Lederer is saying is that a party joke—no matter how sharp or witty—doesn't work without audience participation. If they don't get it, the illustration falls flat.

Everyone knows the story of the boogeyman and his swooning victim. In the above imaginary *Time* image, the dental metaphors (certainly) and clothing allusions (probably) are well within our global reference (even if we don't know a country's colors, flag–like drapery can be conveyed effortlessly through design and composition).

The concept *must* resonate with our cultural understanding and knowl–edge base, or the high concept flies under our radar. Look . . . can you see it?

HI, CONCEPT!

"I personally love this aspect of illustration," Garrett says. "Many of my clients, like *Business Week, Fortune, Kiplinger's,* and *Smart Money,* also appre–ciate this process. I get a kick working up new ways to show mutual funds and capital investment images."

The challenge, of course, is to come up with an arresting image that will both simplify *and* clarify a complex subject. To do this, the illustrator may start with everyday themes that resonate with him or her personally (and are easily identified by the audience). Ah, but here comes the spin. Now apply a smart, conceptual twist that morphs the setup into something wittier (and more interesting).

"A solid concept always makes a piece of art so much stronger," illus–trator Akiko Stehrenberger will tell you. "Giving the viewer a chance to think a little leads to the 'aha!' moment."

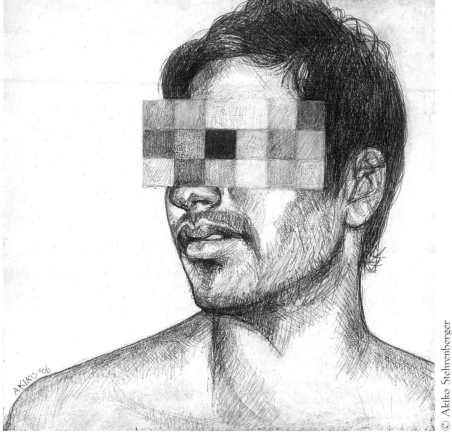

© Akiko Stehrenberger

Why Are These Skills Important?

Illustrators are challenged on multiple levels. Technically and conceptually, we have our work cut out for us. Everyone, from art directors to clients, from readers to critics, will be asking: What's the big idea? What are you attempting with this illustration?

Everyone asks because, with every illustration, you are putting out a statement. That statement is, "Look at me!"

So why should we respond? What's the catch? No catch; but there is a hook, and that hook is the message. What is the illustration about—what are you saying with this art?

Conceptual skills are important for a number of reasons. The illustrator ultimately accepts the responsibility of conveying the message to do a complete job. Concept dictates content and content determines composition.

So, composition, along with value, color, line, texture, pattern, and shape/form are the technical aspects of the concept—all in service to the ultimate goal: Get the message across, tell a story (or just decorate a wall).

Illustration communicates something. Conceptual skills can either spell it out or make you read between the lines, but it's all about communication—and that's quite a hook.

Yin and Yang out the Ying Yang

What's more important: good conceptual abilities or great drawing skills? Now *there's* a debate that could take you into the wee hours. There are folks who argue that this one's a no-brainer—basic talent is paramount. But in direct contrast to that reasonable guideline, I can point out the number of successful working artists who can conceptualize but boast those minimal drawing gifts mentioned earlier.

Certainly, the beginning of the illustration process means getting to the concept of that visual. Once we know where the concept is going, we can play with the toys.

But I'm also from the school that says better skills facilitate a more fluid process and sophisticated technique. So does that put me sitting on a fence, smack in the middle of the road? Oy!

Okay, here's an exercise for you:

Let's go back to our illustration of the Third-World tyrant and his nuclear threat. The nice art director at *Time* says your original Dracula concept is too trite. She wants to consider four other ideas.

She now asks you to present roughs for two black-and-white pieces, plus two full-color works. Black-and-white art *cannot* be a tonal version (or variation) of either color piece—each illustration must address the backstory, and each must boast a unique technical (and conceptual) slant.

So, you must explore four different techniques and examine four new concepts. Not only that, but she specifies that all those overused horror-movie metaphors are strictly off-limits: no monsters, no teeth, no women in jeopardy.

Now, where do you start? Does concept push technique or will technique promote concept? Oh, yes, she wants the roughs by 5:00 Monday, as a final is due by 9:00 Wednesday.

Brainstorming and Ideas

"Brainstorming helps me come up with what's expected and unexpected," says Stehrenberger. "You consider all possibilities—both related and unrelated—then slowly narrow it down to a strong concept. I do it for every project."

Winn-Lederer tells us, "The first image that comes to mind is a little tempest in a teapot." And here, she smiles. "Brainstorming—BS for short—is the essential catalyst in preparing for an assignment."

WHAT IS BRAINSTORMING?

Brainstorming is both a mental diversion and a physical activity, each feeding into the other. You may play the process out in your head or on paper. It could be a completely spontaneous, freeform exercise.

Perhaps there is a recreational quality to your method. You doodle and daydream; climb aboard a fast-moving train of thought; word and picture play lead to deeper word and picture association—the fun and immediacy of the game sparks the intellectual process.

For others, brainstorming must be pondered at length. For some folks, it is this deliberate organization of ideas that provides the key (and outlines, charts, or diagrams become crucial tools).

Here's another exercise for you:

A. Pick a topic, any topic.

1. Draw for thirty minutes; focus totally on this subject matter. Everything you draw must relate to this topic only.

2. Clear your head completely; don't have *anything* in mind. With pen in hand, just start to draw. Anything. Draw spontaneously for at least thirty minutes.

3. Make a phone call and gab (again, for at least thirty minutes); scribble constantly while you chat.

4. Crank up your favorite band on the iPod, and let the music take your pen over.

5. Click on the television (or watch a movie on DVD). Keep the sound on. Make sure you draw to both a comedy and then a drama (our thirty-minute rule still applies). Now, make it a point to watch something utterly boring; draw to that.

"I would have you know now that I'd been happy. I made the best illuminations in Our Sultan's workshop; no one could rival my mastery. Through the work I did privately I earned nine hundred silver coins a month, which naturally only makes all of this even harder to bear. I was responsible for painting and embellishing books. I illuminated the edges of pages coloring their borders with the most lifelike designs of looks, branches, flowers and birds. I painted scalloped Chinese clouds, clusters of overlapping vines and forests of color that hid gazelles, galleys, sultans, trees, palaces, horses and hunters. In my youth I would decorate a plate or the back of a mirror or a chest or at times the ceiling of a mansion or of a Bosphorus manor or even a wooden spoon. In later years however I only worked on manuscript pages because Our Sultan paid well for them. I can't say it seems insignificant now. You know the value of money even when you are dead."
— Orhan Pamuk, My Name is Red
2001

6. Repeat step 5 of the exercise. Different shows. Draw with the sound *off*. What's coming up for you?

B. Now, pick a topic, something you know inside and out.

1. Organize your thoughts on paper—words only. Determine your direction through a written outline (a list or spreadsheet are other alternatives here). Document what you know about this topic and write out a script for a subsequent drawing based on this knowledge base. Do the drawing based on this outline.

2. Visually organize your drawing via a map, flowchart (or pie chart), or diagram. Do the drawing based on this organization.

3. Organize your thoughts on 3" × 5" cards—words only. Organize the cards (on a bulletin board, or the floor) and dope out a drawing with these notes.

4. Organize your thoughts on 3" × 5" cards—pictures only. Organize the cards (again, on a bulletin board, or the floor) and do another drawing based on the flash cards.

What's clicking?

Says Winn-Lederer: "BS for an artist is akin to the process an actor employs for a one-person performance: arranging the staging area, reviewing the script, applying makeup, or adjusting a costume."

Thinking on paper is most effective for illustrator and educator Matt McElligott. "I try to make a beeline from every idea to my hand, with no detours," he says. "If I can remove my conscious mind from the process, interesting things start to happen.

"The problem comes when that voice in my head says, 'Nah, better not, it'll never fly.' When my 'editing brain' butts in, he plugs up the works. Good ideas never get the chance to grow and develop, and fear of failure takes over."

For Winn–Lederer, brainstorming can translate into wandering around her studio or the neighborhood, moving through daily routines while thinking directly and indirectly about the project at hand.

Your computer screen, that old chalkboard, paper napkins from lunch— even the backs of envelopes—are all legitimate vehicles for brainstorming. You can do it solo. You can brainstorm with a partner, or in a group—face-to-face or over the phone.

I HEARD IT THROUGH THE GRAPEVINE

And these days, you certainly can do it electronically. "When flipping images around for input from others," Winn–Lederer comments, "e-mail is wonderful."

"And I actually utilize the Internet search engines," Stehrenberger adds. "I type in adjectives related to the original idea and see where it takes me."

When I Googled "brainstorming online," I got a wealth of great hits. All boasted titles like The Idea Lottery, Free the Genie (really more of a product, and not a standalone Web site), and Random Word Generator (to list only three). Most sites offered fresh insights into problem-solving and provided innovative—and interactive—creative play. This was fun brainstorming that was nonexistent before the rise of the Web (which itself is arguably *the* brainstorm of the last quarter century).

Looking at the work of other illustrators is a grand form of brainstorming. "This is fine motivation," says McElligott. "There's nothing quite like double servings of inspiration and humble pie to light the creative fires.

"One of my favorite places to check out what other illustrators are up to is Drawn! (*www.drawn.ca*), a blog run by a bunch of Canadian illustrators. Every day they spotlight several artists, and there's always something there to encourage and impress."

Other great resources (to name only a few) are IllustrationMundo, Sandbox, and Cartoon Brew. YouTube offers a profusion of illustrators' video step-by-step tutorials. These art-in-action demos are wonderful learning opportunities, available 24/7 with only a few clicks of your mouse.

Like Stehrenberger and McElligott, Winn-Lederer keeps dual passports in the real and virtual worlds for research and reference. "Depending on the deadline, brainstorming also means hours online (or at the library) sifting through images and ideas until a clear mental image forms," she says.

I DON'T KNOW WHAT IT IS, BUT I LIKE IT

What is the outcome, or "supposed" to be the outcome? Simply said: a strong concept! Stehrenberger notes that subtle, unexpected details that enhance an image (and prop up the editorial) are often the direct result of brainstorming.

"Brainstorming helps me to *not* always think in a straight line," she comments. "Thoughts lead to other thoughts. Ridiculous ideas can lead to logical ones. Brainstorming adds something special to my illustrations."

Here's an example of how an off-kilter idea can lead to a viable concept. In the middle of brainstorming a greeting card assignment, an illustrator has a heated disagreement with his wife—provoked, he complains, entirely by his spouse.

The argument isn't pretty, but once some of dust settles, the encounter generates a clever idea for a birthday card based on a classic sci-fi movie the artist loved as a kid.

He researches the original movie poster online and immediately draws a parody of the film based on the flick's iconic image. Juggling only a few words (in the title), the illustrator comes up with *Attack of the 50-Year-Old Woman*.

Advice and Critique

Input from an outside source—advice and/or critique—is an invaluable (and inevitable) part of the illustration game, every step of the way.

You are in business, and *on the job* (and as such, you obviously must please a client or employer). But why not take advantage of other critically honest eyes and objective, independent perspectives?

In the middle of a job, think of feedback as an education for you and the client—input and output. It goes both ways, right? As a kid, when I was having a problem with somebody, my mom would always tell me to communicate. Actually, she would say, "You have a big mouth—use it! And exactly *what* are those ears for, Mickey?" Mom was a primo teacher and a wonderful art director.

It's the exchange that counts. Don't let your ego do the talking for you. It's about the art, not about you. Yes, have your own mind and speak your truth. Certainly educate your client (or colleague, or teacher, or whomever).

But *listen* and learn. It's not about your self-image; it's about making the best illustration you can.

Welcome candid contributions whenever (and from wherever) you can. As McElligott says, "Better to find someone who has absolutely no interest in stroking your ego, someone who's not afraid to tell you exactly what he thinks. Outside of clients and art directors, these people are extremely hard to find. The trick is to get feedback from someone who will give it to you straight, and whose opinions you value."

Getting Unstuck

What if the ideas aren't coming, or you can't get motivated? Maybe it's simply not working. When you are stuck or stalled, there are ways to jump-start your ideas, to hotwire the creative process. Here are a few:

Motivation gurus often call you to tap into your inner strength (a favored mantra being, "I am good enough"). Employing a nice bit of self-help, Winn-Lederer might review her own portfolio or reread her own résumé (effective because, after all, you *are* good enough).

She'll talk to a friend or head to the coffee shop with a sketchbook. She may look at portfolios on the Web "to see what others are doing." Sometimes, she picks up a dictionary or encyclopedia and opens to a random page. "Life is such a crap-shoot; no one technique works consistently, so you have to trust your instincts."

Illustrator Sarajo Frieden goes for walks in her neighborhood, where the streets are "filled with signs in at least three languages I can't understand (Thai, Armenian, Korean). It's this proximity to divergent and diverse cultures which has always made me feel most at home.

"The hand-painted signs and shop murals remind me of being in Mexico—of traveling, of celebrating the handmade and making do with what

you have. Sometimes I will draw from these letter forms, or from the inter—
esting characters I have gotten to know or recognize during my sojourns."

© Chris Spollen

Sketchbooks, Journals, Diaries

Chris Spollen suggests you maintain a regular sketchbook or a journal.
This he labels "vital in finding your voice, vision, or style."

"Whenever I have to attend a meeting or a lecture, or anywhere where
I won't be in total darkness, I bring along a sketchbook," Frieden tells us. She
points out that her sketchbook is not fancy or precious in any way. "Make
[your sketchpad] out of coffee—shop napkins and staple them together if you
like drawing on that."

Winn—Lederer is another sketchbook advocate: "I sketch all the time.
Sketchbooks are convenient and allow spontaneity of expression. The
numerous journals I have filled over the years are mostly small and discreet
and fit in a purse or pocket.

"I take them traveling, and write or draw in them every day. These have become a treasure trove of ideas from which I've developed many unique pieces of art."

Frieden feels her best drawing is done when someone "drones on in the background. And if they are saying something interesting, it sometimes finds its way into the drawings."

For Frieden (and many of our colleagues), the point of sketching is play. "Like yoga or any discipline," she says, "I want to build time into my day and wander via my drawings or paintings. The portability of a sketchbook is a great way to carve out time to do this.

"I try not to be too self-conscious about what I'm doing. Some people call this flow. It's a wonderful state of being. This is my 'practice.'"

Practice, Product, and Process

These are inextricably intertwined. I don't believe a quality product can emerge full-grown from anyone's forehead.

Practice builds mechanical skills—eye/hand coordination—as well as conceptual skills. Drawing more (and drawing often) will improve your way with a pencil and make your mind and heart open to visits from the muse of inspiration.

Which brings us to an excellent question: Do you practice? Do you *need* to practice? Is getting to Carnegie Hall, as the old joke tells it, all a simple matter of practice, practice, practice (and then more practice)?

Says Ilene Winn-Lederer: "Drawing is no different than dancing or performing music in that both require extensive discipline of muscle and memory. And like language skills, if you don't use 'em, you lose 'em.

"So the answer is yes, it's important to draw every day, even if it's just a doodle while you are on the phone."

Like riding a bike, I think practice is all about balance—in this instance, the balance of time, energy, and hand skills. And like riding a bike, the knack doesn't just disappear if you somehow drop the exercise of drawing.

But not drawing for a time can definitely put you out of balance. You may swerve somewhat until you get up to speed. "When I am occasionally constrained by circumstances from drawing for a time," Winn-Lederer admits, "I can tell you that it takes no small amount of time to regain the coordination necessary for full expression."

My advice: Just get back on the bike.

PRACTICE MAKES PERFECT?

"Unfortunately, practice doesn't always make *my* work *perfect*," says Garrett. "But it does seem to smooth out the process of creating for me," he adds.

Garrett follows a regular ritual that maintains hand skills and exercises his mind, to boot. "I keep a little orange notebook where I jot down notes and observations," he says. "Sometimes I record conceptual metaphors for later use. For example, last August I saw this kid on a cool bike. I quickly drew this in my sketchbook and noticed that the shape of the wheels looked like daisy flowers. This new metaphor helped me a few months later while doing an assignment for the *Wall Street Journal*. Even though the final illustration was slightly different from that initial drawing, the idea was first planted in my sketchbook."

Garrett finds that such observational drawing also helps to limber his eye/hand coordination. "While these finished drawings are nothing to write home about," he says, "they help me loosen up and see new things. I might sketch stuff from memory or jot down a dream. Drawings could be based on conversations overhead at Starbucks. Sometimes they are purely decorative doodles that later morph into real objects or become background patterns and textures for my collages."

DISCIPLINE

Do you lament your "lack of discipline"? What exactly does this mean? The word "discipline" is a land mine of definitions. You can spin those expressions to reflect positive or negative characterizations, so I'm going to steer you toward another word: practice.

As Garrett points out, regular practice can open a window of creativity that fires you up and supplies wonderful artistic direction. "Writers seem to get this," he points out. "Writers know that the process of writing *something*— no matter how lame—will eventually lead to bigger and better ideas."

"I am constantly short of ideas," Garrett reveals. "In the morning, when I first pick up a pencil and start to draw, my first concepts are shamefully awful. Eventually, as I work through the sketches I see some connections growing and greater ideas begin to develop."

Garrett encourages this practice with his students. One of his favorite projects challenges his class to illustrate the concept of "Electricity." "I choose this topic because it is open to a full range of possibilities, from abstract symbols to realistic and/or historical themes," Garrett says. "Students are asked to come up with twenty-five thumbnail concept sketches. At first, the students are frustrated, and think they can only crunch out five good ideas. After working with them for a few minutes, they start to see how some of the thumbnail sketches can lead to other possibilities and more creative solutions."

Are art supplies and materials any part of this mix? Sure. "I'm always on the lookout for new and interesting materials and/or papers," Winn–Lederer says. "Inspiration comes often during a cruise through an art supply shop."

Although she has "pretty much settled on the media I prefer," Winn–Lederer is "always searching for that more perfect version of pen, ink, water–colors, or paper that will both make my job easier and contribute to a more beautiful finished product. I am also committed to using only archival prod–ucts because a client will often ask to purchase the original art."

But on the other hand, there's an old saw that tells it like is: "It's a poor workman who blames his tools." Your materials obviously affect your art process; it is, after all, the utensil that makes the mark. But it is your hand that guides the instrument.

I encourage you to try out new and different art materials. Here's an exercise to spark this exploration:

Do fifty lines in ten days—five per day. Your output can certainly be adapted (up or down, more or less) to fit your personal, professional, or aca–demic schedule. The goal is to get into a routine, a discipline. Can you stay with it?

Do the exercise for a set period of time—say, thirty minutes—so some organization and planning can only help your session.

Maintain the assignment as a *sketchbook* (call it a journal or visual diary, as you like). Any size is fine.

Make the assignment as easy or challenging as your deadline allows. Basically, just draw a long line (or multilines) across the page. Bleed edge to edge; start and stop your stroke past the borders of the page. Work for full arm movement; sweep your hand across the page.

Employ a different tool and/or media *on each page*. Dip a separate brush in another bottle of ink or tube of paint *every page*. Grab another utensil every page. Mix and match. The idea is to see how a certain brush holds a particular ink or paint; to contrast grades of pencils; to compare different brands of colored pencils; to find the difference between cutting and tearing paper, etc.— the interaction of material and page on a daily basis.

Do "enough" of these and you are soon creating highly individual strokes—your unique line signature (aka line character). Eventually, you'll see a spontaneous variation in line weight, and the control, speed, and power that comes from practice. The exercise provides a good lesson in choice and action, application and observation, motion and direction.

DA BLUES

In a chapter about tools, techniques, and concepts, let's wrap up with some nostalgia about just that.

"Sometimes manufacturers discontinue good tools and we are forced to substitute," Winn–Lederer laments. "Case in point, I used a wonderful sumi brush marker made by Sakura for many years until they discontinued making that tool. Though the company has other similar products, they are just not the same. So I switched to different media altogether. Ironically, I am now getting requests for work done in the style afforded by that sumi brush marker. Time to punt."

I also loved this same wonderful marker and sorely lamented its passing. By the way, Ilene may have had to punt, but she notes that staying in the game is what really counts. And that's exactly what we've been discussing . . . good tools, smart ideas, and sharp skills (all in the right hands: yours).

Stylin'

Style is the packaging for flair and creativity. Often, the three terms are interchanged, mixed and matched. But style isn't the ultimate goal and certainly shouldn't be your *grail*.

"Style and technique is something that always stirred my brain," says Scott Bakal. "But it's not how it comes out that's important. Every time I sit down, I think about how I can achieve that next level of creativity in my work. If you are as creative as you can be, just produce the work you want to make—you will find a style (and a market for it)."

"And your mistakes, accidents, and wrong turns are really a crucial part of this creative process," David Julian joins in. "There's just not one way to look at things, never a single way to do it."

"After thirty-plus years of doing illustration," illustrator Robin Jareaux says, picking up this thread, "I have watched different styles go in and out of style. And that is all I did, *watched it*—from airbrush (in the late seventies) to digital now.

"Different styles will come and go. If you have the basic background of knowing how to draw well, you will always be in style."

Illustrator Rick Tulka agrees. Asked about changing his style after he found his direction, Tulka says he never changed. "I was happy with what I was doing. Even with different styles coming and going, I never felt there was a need to change. I only wanted to improve what *I* was doing."

"Style is not the thing to aspire to," Paul Dallas adds. "Although it sounds pretentious, acquiring a 'vision' is far more worthy of one's efforts and transcends the limited shelf life implied by any one particular 'style.'

"Vision," he says, "suggests an original outlook and sensibility that acts as a constant when the work is permitted to evolve technically over time. 'Vision' tends to yield mark-making that is more authentic and genuine, and, as such, holds up better and longer than mere 'style.'"

Finally, there's always the ol' style-over-substance debate. Illustrator Steve Hughes suggests we borrow from the good book of Yogi (Berra): "Illustration style," he paraphrases, "is 90 percent mental; the other half is physical."

5
It's Just
Business

*Answer certain questions: "Does my
illustration fit my audience? This is a
commission; am I hitting the client's target?"
That's our "business."*

—GIOVANNI DA RE, ILLUSTRATOR;
  VITTORIO VENETO, ITALY

The State of the Organization   The industry is going through quite a transitional phase—the digital revolution and the rise of the Internet have radically altered illustration practice, structure, and philosophy (and that's putting it mildly).

Elsewhere in this book we examine some of those big transformations. Here we'll talk about organizing and running an illustration business in this day and age—just, uh, for a change.

A Business Model

"My mother was the art side, my father was the business side," says John Dykes when asked about his business education. "As I was going

through school, my father was always stressing the importance of the business side. Going into illustration, he was always asking me, 'Syracuse University—do they have any business models or business plans you can follow?'

"I've always been interested in the business end of things," Dykes adds. "I love the idea of commerce, and the self-promotion side. I find a lot of energy in doing things that I think will lead to business. It fires something inside of me."

If anything, your business model must be what Dykes labels a "well-worked machine." (You may have heard the expression as "a well-oiled machine." Either way, the thinking definitely rings true.) No matter what state the current "state of the art" is in, or what direction marketing changes take you, an illustrator will need to establish a functional business model to put the practice of illustration to work.

A plan. The plan. What's *your* business plan for the next year? How about five years? Mapping out where you want your business to go is just plain smart. Organizing an action strategy to meet that goal—on a daily, monthly, and yearly basis—is only wise.

This written manifesto can be on the back of a business card or the size of *War and Peace*, but do it. A business plan is the personal, professional, and financial yardstick that gives you a place to start, helps you focus, and fosters growth.

It's rather a straightforward proposition: Understand your objectives, know your mission, state your goals, take action; revise accordingly. What do you really want and why?

A Model Business

One component of a good business plan is setting up shop, hopefully creating a work environment you enjoy—an affordable, professional space that's right for you. In reality, this can be anywhere you can get the work done: at home in a studio down the hall, or at the office across town.

Now, in terms of stuff: You must realistically assess—and then choose—what you actually need, what you can afford, and what will fit into your space.

Before you gear up for that first day of business, you'll want to get a handle on what to do before your doors open. Visit your accountant; see your lawyer. Create your first promotional piece, as well as business forms, cards, and letterhead. Signage? Do you need any permits and licenses? Is a rent deposit (or mortgage) looming? Phone and phone lines? Utilities?

Don't forget the keys to the place.

Now consider your financial plan. Of course you don't want to start out underfinanced, but you don't want to overspend either. The idea of a financial plan is to weigh the money you need, how much you can realistically earn, and, if needed, where (and how) to get financing. You'll also want to create a working budget to maintain cash flow and keep your business in the black.

A financial plan begins with figuring out what your startup expenses will be, then doping out monthly expenses (that obviously add up to yearly expenditures). Now you'll compare earnings with expenditures.

Mock up a budget. Have it on paper. At some point you'll have to balance costs and income to see if your business plan is viable. Can you make ends meet? Are you turning a profit?

The plan also entails knowing where you're finding the needed money to get your business off the ground. Is it the bank or credit union or a commercial finance or credit company? Personal reserves (savings) and/or resources (an insurance policy, credit card)? Spouse, family and/or friends; a business partner of some kind?

Consider hiring (or at the very least, consulting) an accountant. This expert could very well become the key player in your business plan, especially in regards to doing your income taxes. Personal tax preparation is elaborate enough. Business taxes? Oy! From my experience, a good accountant is well worth every penny. Run, don't walk, to the yellow pages.

Starting Up

The problem with starting a business (and that includes freelancing) might just be *security*. Pesky questions like, "Will there be enough work to keep me afloat? Where's my next gig coming from? Can I really cut it?" are common to all startups, no matter what business you're in.

Maybe you feel good business just breaks down to a simple concept: organization—recognizing responsibilities, prioritizing, and then getting busy.

Yes. Business management *is* about targeting priorities and juggling people, services, time, and expenses. As a startup, it's good to recognize that *effective* business management means superior organization, establishing systems and procedures, and maintaining good records and files on all aspects of your business.

Rapport—people skills—factor into all this. Frequently meeting and candidly dealing with clients. Informing. Educating. This is how you build a history with clients and establish a reputation. The word *service* is certainly an important part of the vocabulary.

> *I'll make a distinction between an "illustrator" and an "artist" (at least in a "Bohemian" sense). But I'll make that distinction only in the context that an illustrator is called on to solve visual problems, using skill and creativity to communicate or translate a concept into a product.*
> —GIOVANNI DA RE, ILLUSTRATOR;
> VITTORIO VENETO, ITALY

This all sounds like *communication* to me. And that's what you do best. You're a communicator. You solve communication problems. You're *good* at this.

Mindset

Sports analogies make my wife laugh—all the "guy talk" she says I babble during my conversations, especially. I'm no athlete or closet jock, and even though I risk the light wrath of the goddess, I say the "game plan" concept is a good one.

Is it remotely possible to think about business planning as a serious, but fun—even creative—necessity? If you can, organizing your business goals may not drive you crazy when you realize you're involved in a fun, creative, but serious *business* venture.

Let me qualify, however. I don't know if "playing the game right" means making a lot of money, for, as illustrator Ali Douglass comments, "You know, I have a life and I want to be self-sufficient. I want to grow more; I want to *do* more (personally and professionally).

"I think it is important to write the plan down, or at least to have some clear idea of what 'it' is—what *you* want, because otherwise you just float through life. An idea on paper somehow means it's more 'official'—somehow, more obtainable."

OH, DID I SAY THAT OUT LOUD?

"One year, I made the declaration to my parents that I intended to make [X amount of dollars]," Douglass continues. "I think my folks thought I was crazy, because I said, 'This is the year, Dad.' And he was thinking, 'My God, child, how are you going to reach that?'

"But he was also proud of me, if for no other reason than that I established the goal and I set out to do it. And do it, by the way, with a positive attitude.

"And I did it. I just kind of kept saying to myself, 'I want to make [X amount of dollars], and I want to have more work this year,' and I pulled it off." Here, Douglass pauses and says candidly, "Now, a sunny outlook alone is no guarantee of success, but I think it helps to *get it in your mind* and start subliminally thinking of what you have to do in order to reach your objective."

Simple advice: Keep the prize in front of you and head right for it. And if it doesn't work out, then revise the idea and go for plan B or C. A good end run was always part of the original design, right?

Money Matters

It's important at startup to keep tabs on finances. Separate your business and personal bank accounts. Keep organized, fastidious financial records (and learn how to maintain clear-cut books for you and/or your accountant's sake).

Be on top of what you have to do for the IRS and when. Plan for future growth. Invest in your retirement *now* (even at startup).

Have good, comprehensive business (as well as personal) insurance. As a freelancer, health insurance will be costlier, but *don't pass on it* (and do buy disability insurance—yes, at startup). Health insurance is absolutely necessary—do your research. Spend the money, but shop around. Purchase the best coverage you can afford.

Plan Ahead

"Think ahead of the curve—have a five-year plan," Dan Yaccarino advises. "And try to map out the current year, as well."

Yaccarino will admit that this is a relatively recent strategy for him, too, and that it has everything to do with the illustrator examining his business and wanting more of a direction for his long-term ventures. "I sat myself down and said, 'Okay, where have you come from? What were your accomplishments? Where do you want to go?'

Kick-Start Your Business Thinking

This chapter hopes to help aspiring illustrators develop their own business plans. Here's an exercise—just a simple set of ten questions—to initiate such a plan.

1. What kind of illustration have you been doing this last year?

2. What kind of illustration have you been doing the last five years?

3. What kind of illustration would you like to do in the next year?

4. Where do you see the state of the illustration business in five years?

5. What kind of illustration will you be doing five years from now?

6. What can you do *artistically* to make this happen? This month . . . this quarter . . . this year? (Write it down. Do it! Repeat this exercise every twelve months.)

7. What can you do *businesswise* to make this happen? This month . . . this quarter . . . this year? (Write it down. Do it! Repeat this exercise every twelve months.)

8. What can you do in terms of *research and development* to make this a reality? This month . . . this quarter . . . this year? (Write it down. Do it! Repeat this exercise every twelve months.)

9. What can you do in terms of *marketing and promotion* to make this happen? This month . . . this quarter . . . this year? (Write it down. Do it! Repeat this exercise every twelve months.)

10. What can you do in terms of *networking* to make this happen? This month . . . this quarter . . . this year? (Research. Make contacts. Repeat this exercise every twelve months.)

"It's being conscious of the projects on the back burner *and* in progress, thinking ahead to the future and priorities. It's also being aware of what isn't working as the plan progresses and eliminating those things."

When asked about business planning, Klauba takes a sensible, generic tact. "I discovered for myself that something that feels right (or sounds logical)—*anything* I can somehow apply to my business—sticks with me; I'll use it.

"Every December or January, I'll sit down and write out my upcoming yearly plan. I try to coordinate this with my long-term planning. It's important to keep short-term strategy *and* long-term goals in mind. Figuring all this out helps you stay focused. Not just creatively, but personally, as well."

And how does Klauba nurture this marketing approach? "First and foremost," Klauba says, "I know that you must create a really strong body of work that you can confidently offer publishers or designers.

"Right now, I think my art is just where I want it to be, but I want to craft a larger library—a mass of new work that might take another three to five years to make. This is a long-term goal I am actively pursuing."

© Dan Yaccarino

End Game

As Paul Melia says, "Organization is not the enemy of creativity." To which Dan Yaccarino adds, "Realize that this is a profession. An industry. You must always have a mind to do this—and 'do it right.'"

6

Life Skills

The ability to deal with an ever-changing world is exactly where our creative survival resides.

—CHRIS SPOLLEN, ILLUSTRATOR

Do the Grind   So you want to be an illustrator? "Well, it's certainly an interesting and enjoyable lifestyle," illustrator Chris Spollen states.

Indeed it is. For me, being an illustrator is quite like hitting a buffet table of immense riches and challenges. And for Spollen, a veteran professional, the most important item on the menu is passion. "Your passion is what will define you," he declares. But let's assume that the zeal for what you do is a given. Not every day brings fame and fortune—but you still must deal with the guts and glory of your everyday schedule.

In this chapter we will examine the mix of skills you need to balance a vital life at and away from the drawing board. How does a busy profes-

sional maintain business as usual *and* sustain himself/herself—plus home and family?

This is perhaps the most fundamental question, as a rounded life is the goal.

Set Up the Shop

One key aspect that profoundly affects your routine is establishing and maintaining a work space. The location of your studio is truly your first real order of business.

Chances are you will establish your "shop" in your house or apartment, but it's not a given. And what about the great home–studio debate? Yep, this is a good one.

"Tough question," illustrator Darren Booth admits. "So far, I've always worked out of my house, and the lines are definitely blurred—sometimes for better and sometimes for worse. What I'm learning is that it doesn't matter where I am physically to do the work, but mentally I need to be in 'my space.'"

Are these separate concepts? Should they be? How sacred is our concept of "home"? How dedicated are we to the idea of the "workplace"? Perched on our sharply cut edge, smack in the middle of this techno-age, have we blurred the lines (for better or for worse)?

"I have always had a home studio," comments illustrator Tuko Fujisaki. "For the most part this has been a separate room (or two). When I lived in New Mexico, I had the luxury of having a separate room for computer stuff!

"But this can get a little fuzzy, as I will sometimes work out on the deck, or at another table totally removed from the studio proper. When I'm just conceptualizing or at the sketch stage, I can work anywhere."

You can work to live, or you can live to work. I prefer the former.
—DARREN BOOTH, ILLUSTRATOR

"Once upon a time, the concept of home versus studio was difficult for my family and friends to understand," Booth reveals. "They acknowledged my situation, but the fact that I could work out of my house was suspect. They had trouble seeing that I didn't have to go to a workplace to make money.

"If I traveled to a studio space, my family may not have questioned it. It was very frustrating at the time. Plus, all of a sudden, I became the guy who was always home and could work 'whenever he wanted.' Unexpected visits, phone calls, requests for help, etc., became a common and annoying occurrence. Because I was at home, I was treated like I wasn't working!

"This was resolved by not answering the door or phone while I was working. But other solutions under consideration at the time were: pinching, punching, kicking, and screaming; biting, scratching, snarling, and salivating. However, it's all smooth sailing now."

Tune In, Tune Out

As Booth's tale points out, your space should be a spot where you can tune out the world and its distractions. "Concentration is very important. Most art is usually created in quiet," Spollen adds.

Certainly, a place that promotes your absolute focus is an important factor. But that will only be one part of the mix. When choosing a place to work, what does one have to consider besides distractions?

There are, of course, the standard concerns of locating (or relocating) anywhere: climate and locale (including the environmental, social, cultural, and political ambiance). City or country? Is this a long-term relocation or short-term move? Is this place "just to start" or your "I'm putting down roots, this is my dream come true" spot?

How's the cost of living? If you're not working at home, what is your mode of transportation? Schools for the kids? Recreation and enter-tainment? Facilities (shopping, civic services) for one and all (personally and professionally)?

If you are working at home, how much room do you really need (and how much space do you honestly have)? If you are working outside the home, are we talking private or shared office space? Rent and utilities? Commute? Amenities? Access?

And we shouldn't assume that your gig is as a *freelance* illustrator, and that you work out of the home (or out of a private, outside office). Saying that, the days of the bustling illustration studios are indeed long gone, but a pocket of such shops can still be found.

However, if you're working part- or full-time at a studio (big or small), it's probably as a graphic designer with appreciable illustration chops (and you've been hired as such). So, as with any job anywhere, the generic con-siderations listed above are just as valid.

So you found your Batcave. What do you do with all the bats? "This may sound like a right–brain/left–brain thing," Spollen says, "but I find a daily to–do list is imperative."

And Greg Nemec sees Spollen's point. "Chris is saying that keeping a to–do list may seem antithetical to what a creative person does, but it's necessary," Nemec clarifies. "It's a really important point, crucial for people like me, who may have come out of art school romanticizing what we are doing and don't want to be as earthbound as an office manager may be."

Agreed! There are often way too many things for my little pea brain to hold, but I can follow a list like nobody's business. Maybe I'm a little ADHD. I just know that if the task is on paper, I'm on it. And if you are goal–oriented at all (like me), you get a wee, wee, little buzz when you check items off that list.

You may prefer to go electronic here. PDAs are handy and come with a range of features at various price points. But the list (analog or digital) is an ongoing thing. Think rollover. Items that do not get crossed off that particular workday go onto the following day's list (and you pick up from there). "Organizing your time is key to getting the most out of that day," Spollen tells us.

Sure, this is elementary—but invaluable—advice. So simple, we may blow it off to concentrate on the broad strokes of motivational tapes and business seminars. Listen to this down–to–earth wisdom. It works.

It's All You

Okay; we're cozy and our ducks are neat in their rows. What else to consider? Well, for one thing, how *does* an illustrator spend his work time? Chances are you will be self–employed. Which means you are essentially a subcontractor, hired by a second or third party (like a magazine, or a designer doing a brochure for a client) to do what you do best: draw.

If you're a freelancer, you are also the office manager and secretary, sales manager and staff, marketing guru and promotional department. You're the maintenance guy and the entire mailroom. Freelancing morphs all those jobs into one. You will juggle and hustle—that's the very nature (and definition) of a one-man (or one-woman) shop.

A big part of your job will be figuring out how to deal: with deadlines, with all the busy bees buzzing around those due dates. We've mentioned two big aspects already: space and organization. Let's complete the trifecta and talk about how you use your time.

TIME

As a freelancer, you won't be punching a time clock, and it's entirely *your* schedule—*you* decide when you go to work (and if you even want to take the time to "dress" for "work").

You determine your actual workday—it's only the proverbial nine-to-five if you say so. Nobody will be watching over your shoulder to make sure you're getting the job done (let alone getting the job done right). To pull that trick off, you'd need a mirror. But that's not a bad idea—find a mirror and greet the (hopefully) tough boss who should be keeping you on task.

But effective time management also means tapping into the spaces between the hard work. Getting away from the board is as important as time spent hunched over that desk.

Gimme a Break

Okay, you're super-organized. You work in a sweet shop which, at times, feels like a sweat shop—you are crazy busy with a steady flow of grand jobs. But consider this: Do you have a life away from the board? Do you live for your work, or vice versa? Does your work define you?

In a vocation where you may have to wear the variety of hats mentioned above (any or all of 'em on any given day), these are awfully pertinent questions. And the answers are even more critical.

"Life feeds work," Paul Dallas says. "Without a life, you will eventually starve for ideas." But as an emerging artist, Dallas made some hard choices. He deliberately avoided long-term commitments because he realized how they could affect his work.

"I also saw how my work, or lack of it, could cause others unwarranted difficulty," he tells us. "It wasn't until I felt reasonably satisfied with my accomplishments as an illustrator that I truly integrated my professional and personal lives—it was only then that I married and started a family."

SECOND SHIFT

For some illustrators, establishing and maintaining a life beyond the board—particularly for the draw-at-home freelancer—becomes another full-time job in itself. And, as Ilene Winn-Lederer will tell you, "Because my art (and yours) can be so addictive, it takes major self-discipline to pull yourself away and attend to your relationships and environment."

But the nimble illustrator figured out the key to making both jobs run smoothly: "You compartmentalize," she says. "Explained as metaphor, you create a room in your mind for each of your responsibilities, and cultivate the ability to mentally monitor each room as needed."

"Working at home is tough," Spollen comments. "A home office kind of molds the idea of the freelance life (as defined by the individual). This generally means putting in longer hours than most folk—the trade-off for doing something you love."

"In my case," Ken Meyer says, "I might sometimes spend a little too much time away from the board. I almost always feel guilty when I am watching television or a movie, out doing something, playing tennis, whatever it may be. But I do think that those times are essential to holding onto your sanity."

"Being a freelance illustrator and writer, I feel that I should always be working," Susanna Pitzer comments. "That is the only way I can get ahead.

"In order to have a family life, social life, even a break during the day, I have learned to put them into my schedule. If it's on the schedule, it's something I'm supposed to do.

"I'll write out a day schedule that includes eating, walking dogs, and talking to my significant other. I know this sounds extreme, but I find it hard to stop working without this little mind trick.

"So just as I use the schedule to get work done, I use the schedule to allow myself to take breaks.

Is this "real work?" Not really. Work is doing something when you'd rather be doing something else.
        —PAUL DALLAS, ILLUSTRATOR

"I also completely leave the city every couple of months. I know everyone can't do that, but you could leave your house for a day. It's amazing how being away from my home and work clears my brain and gives me more ideas, energy. I come back refreshed and ready to go, and my work is better."

"Most mornings are like an obstacle course just to get into my studio," Doug Klauba says with a laugh, "and as soon as I sit down, start to get comfortable at the board, and lift a pencil, I hear my wife calling my name . . . 'Doooouuug.'

"It seems to happen on a daily basis in my home studio. You see, we have two young boys and one is a little over a year old. As this story goes, the little guy just woke from his morning nap at the same time that my wife has gotten out of the shower.

"Now, a few weeks ago it was okay to let him stand in the crib or 'play yard,' but he is now crawling and exploring the house. We can't leave him in the crib because he works hard at climbing out (and we know that one day he will succeed).

"So, work will have to wait for the next forty-five minutes as my wife gets dressed and can relieve me. I have to admit that it can be very frustrating, especially when deadlines loom over my head. And I can't leave the little one alone as he explores the house as he's starting to walk along the furniture and climb everything, which means that he loses his balance and falls a lot.

"He treats my Metro shelving in the studio like a jungle gym, and books are constantly pulled from the shelves and end up on the floor. The work-at-home dad will have to be patient for a little longer, and I do it all with a big smile."

Leggo My Ego

It's all about you, isn't it? Well, just for the moment, let me hear a resounding, guilt-free YES! And for our immediate purposes, it's okay.

But let's be realistic, too. As illustrator Stan Shaw points out, "I wanted to be a star, but the more I studied the history of illustration, the more I found out that there are/were stellar illustrators that are not 'stars.' There are more Fred Pfiffers than Norman Rockwells—but that says nothing about the quality of their work."

"Cliché though it may be," Winn-Lederer continues, "in most industries (including illustration) where stardom is an option, there is usually a personal price to be paid for fame and fortune. It comes in the form of health problems and/or difficult relationships with family and/or friends."

Stress (even good stress) will take its toll. But sure, some rare individuals exist with the ability to lead a "perfectly" balanced life, especially when faced with dramatic crises or those "stars-in-your-eyes" opportunities.

But what both of these illustrators are advocating is to carefully tend the garden of your career. Set reasonable goals as your career develops; let experience prepare you emotionally and physically to handle challenges over time.

"It's nice to be heard and understood in terms of being an artist with a 'day job' and a relationship," says Maggie Suissman. "I definitely feel like this question of success, of even identifying myself as an illustrator (or even more broadly, as an 'artist') is a tricky one.

"Since I do have a very time-consuming job as a teacher, my work as an artist sometimes seems like it's on the back burner. It's tough to say 'I'm an artist' any more than 'I'm a teacher,' since both of them are such a huge part of my life.

"Of course, other areas of life make the question of one's identity even more complex. I find that I am actually getting into a routine where I have the energy left over to work on creative work.

"I'm doing a series of paintings of the kids I teach. So, on a Saturday, I might spend a big chunk of my day painting. I might also do laundry or make brunch with my boyfriend.

"As a girlfriend, a sister, a friend, I have many roles. So time management is a process, but it's not always easy. Sometimes I think, 'I should be painting!' But it's also so important to nurture my relationships with the people I love, not to mention to take care of myself, my home, etc.

"I do lots of yoga, which is a whole other 'identity'—it really helped change my creative perspective. Those parts of my life that are not expressly related to my artwork can often be a direct inspiration for my art."

© Maggie Suissman

To cap this section, Erin Brady Worsham says this: "I never really let go of my identity as an illustrator. Even when I'm acting as wife, mother, or friend, I'm looking at the world through the eyes of an artist. I know all about stress! I reject stress. Nothing is worth that price. It is enough to be a working artist."

Lone Ranger

Because of the solitary nature of our job, we might reasonably wonder if illustrators are inherently loners. Is this ability to "go it alone" a prerequisite to a successful illustration career?

But we're talking two different things here. By definition, being a "loner" means you prefer to be alone. Without getting into the psychology of this, if it's your individual nature to do your art in solitary confinement, so be it. The loner persona may very well be a facet of your character.

"It is very important to be alone with your thoughts and your ideas," Spollen advises. "Many people never permit this state in today's fast-paced world. Once you get used to it, it's quite wonderful, and creating on a daily basis becomes easier and easier.

"Kind of like tuning out the mass chatter and fine-tuning to an almost faint inner broadcast," Spollen tells us, "this voice can take you on wonderful journeys, explorations of pure passion."

"I'm embarrassed to share this analogy about swimming, but I will anyway," Dallas says, grinning. "When racing (and if they plan to win the race), swimmers usually can't afford to lift their heads out of the water to check the position of other swimmers. So, they race against their own record time. If they beat it, they've done their best.

"The same may be said of illustrators, where checking on the competition's progress is detrimental to focusing on your own. I teach, and it has rewarded me with hundreds of friends and acquaintances who are fellow educators, designers, art directors, artists, and alumni. As an illustrator, my network of contacts was more limited. Doing both, I get the benefit of a regular social life and distance away from it.

"But as much as I enjoy the company of people who make me think and laugh, there is nothing more sublime to me than simply doing. That's when you really face up to who you are."

"Working alone is as necessary as breathing for me," Winn-Lederer states. "Yet I am never 'alone.' It's usually my time for scintillating conversations with my subconscious, both for stress relief and for creative adventures.

"Growing up, solitary time to do my work presented a huge challenge; as an adult, having my own studio was a dream come true. With marriage, family, and community demands, the studio soon became too good to be true.

"Now things have come full circle—kids grown, empty nest, and now elderly parent responsibilities. Sigh. And it's still sometimes hard to settle down and focus on the task at hand.

"You know the old saying that you can't be too thin or too rich?" Winn-Lederer asks. "Add to that, you can't have too much solitary time for doing something you love. Yet occasionally, some great art can be created in very little time. Go figure. I guess it's what you do with what you've got that makes you who you are."

Club Jackets

I want to endorse joining (even starting) professional organizations here. As an Iron City expatriate, I'm even going to insert a little plug.

The Pittsburgh Society of Illustrators recently celebrated its tenth anniversary. Begun as a handful of "illo friends" who met at a bar once a month to commiserate, share portfolios, and garner business advice, this group now boasts 125–plus members and has morphed into the fourth–largest Society of Illustrators in the US.

They meet twice a month, once for business, once for social purposes, and actively mount several exhibits each year in different venues. Couldn't something like this work for you on all fronts? For more information, go to *www.pittsburghillustrators.org.*

LEAVE ME ALONE!

"I like nothing more than spending the day at home alone . . . to do whatever I want," Susanna Pitzer admits. "That's my preference, but I never think of myself as a loner.

"I don't ever feel alone (or bored). Of course, I have two dogs that are always home. Still, I think it's a head full of characters, stories, ideas, and projects that keeps me from feeling alone.

"It also helps that my time is divided between time alone and time working with others. However, when I'm in the middle of a project, I am quite happy to not leave my house for days.

"I'm not sure if all successful illustrators and writers are loners," she muses. "My artist friends like to be alone to get work done, but I still know plenty of people who feel like chewing the wallpaper when they're home for any length of time. So, *liking* to be alone definitely helps the illustrator."

"Being home with two kids doesn't give me much 'alone' time," Meyer tells us. "I have time to myself while they are in school—and I am not at classes of my own—or after they have gone to bed (if I'm not unwinding with my wife).

"But sometimes the pressure builds to be so productive during those times that I feel overwhelmed. And, as I said earlier, the mere fact that I am home sometimes leads people to believe I have free time that can be spent away from my art.

"As it is, I do a large amount of the housework, which can sometimes conflict with deadlines. But you learn to work with it, and hopefully make it work for you. I don't need total isolation to do illustration, but it is much easier to accomplish thumbnails, concept sketches, things like that, without distractions or interruptions."

"After teaching for ten years with students breathing down my neck," David Bowers says, "I dreamt of a day that I could work alone in a studio.

"I love working alone in my studio day after day; I wouldn't have it any other way. Although by the end of the week, I'm ready to see some friends and unwind. As a fine artist now for the last couple of years, I find that I do miss my phone ringing with projects from art directors and the relationships that developed with some of them. It is definitely a little bit lonelier in the fine art world versus the illustration world."

A Good Fit

How's your health, your mental, physical, and emotional well-being? As Winn-Lederer reminds us, "Illustration is a demanding master, and we often ignore our physical and emotional needs when in its thrall."

For me, it comes down to the three stooges, uh, *stages*: relaxation, exercise (plus diet), and play. All three (often combined) are crucial—especially for illustrators. You're only a stooge if you don't promote your good health.

The following is all old news, but absolutely true. I'd bet you know all this (and probably admit it when your mom's not around).

Fact 1: Illustrators *must* exercise—you have to fit it in. We all need to embrace some sort of physical activity, but ya gotta get yer butt *off the chair*, get away from that drawing desk, and *move*—move more than just your wrists. For, as any decent rep will tell you, you are more than just a wrist, right?

"I discovered swimming," Winn-Lederer says. "I would paddle around underwater as a child and young adult but did not learn to swim properly until I turned forty. It has now become a necessity for better mental and physical health.

Meyer plays tennis on a regular (and organized league) basis. "However," he comments, "that also can cause problems at home. Even though I need the release that comes (both physically and mentally) from the sport, certain situations arise. It's, 'Why am I playing tennis when I should be working?' 'Why am I playing tennis when I should be at home with the family?' That eternal guilt factor crops up when I am 'just playing.'"

"Back problems are troublesome for illustrators," Darren Booth comments. "Getting up from the table or computer at least every fifteen minutes to stretch is great. Sometime standing up and working helps a bit. Going to the gym and doing exercises that will strengthen your whole back helps a lot.

"Going to the gym and just getting out of the studio is good for the mind as well," he continues. "A few friends of mine work for a multimedia company, making Web sites, etc. Their employer brings in a yoga instructor once a week to help them with stretches, and they all notice a huge improvement in the way they feel. I am strongly considering this line of action as well."

Bowers lifts weights three days a week and thinks this is one of the best forms of exercise. "It burns calories, relieves stress, and, of course, makes you stronger.

"It's very difficult to find the time to go to a gym," he points out. " So I invested in gym equipment a little at a time until I put together a complete gym. It is much easier to find the time when your gym is in your home. I recently read that 88 percent of people with gym memberships never use the facility to work out."

Spollen also works out on home equipment. He tells us, "As I age, I am convinced that exercise (among other things) promotes creativity."

Fact 2: Man (or woman) does not live by board alone. You are obliged to pursue outside interests; we should actively seek diversion. In reality, you are not actually indentured to Photoshop. You can take a break.

Likewise, you must figure out how to chill (down *or* out). It's not the stress that rocks and rolls our lives—it's how we deal with that tension.

Pitzer walks her dogs in the morning. "We take a long walk in the park or to the library; maybe we go for ice cream. I also make it a point to talk to my niece on the phone."

And like Meyer, Pitzer loves to go to the movies, but (also like Meyer) she stopped going, thinking, "That's time I should be working. Finally, I realized that going to a movie would give me a great break. In the movie theater I can't work. I have no choice but to sit, relax, and give my mind and body a rest.

"I do, however, get to the theater early so I can actually work a bit until the movie comes on.

As for Pitzer and Meyer, movies and television play a part in many illustrators' relaxation time. Listening to and/or playing music is another beloved escape for most artists I know.

Watching and/or participating in sports is an important steam valve for many illustrators, as are organized or solo sports, games, and activities of all varieties. It doesn't much matter; it's both the mental and/or physical exercise that counts.

Erin Brady Worsham says there's nothing like a good dose of day-dreaming to free your mind and temporarily escape the hassles of your life (as well as spark design and concepts).

Let's repeat the message about yoga, and not forget meditation and massage, reading books and magazines, and volunteering. Even shopping—window, or otherwise. All function as great diversions.

Fact 3: Sleep and food are vastly underrated. Your mother knew what she was talking about. It goes without saying that adequate rest and good eating habits are paramount to your personal and creative health. This should be a no-brainer, but many illustrators (young guns and old hands) still try to defy time, nature, and gravity.

"Going to bed and eating during the same hours each day will lead to the ideal creative output," Spollen counsels. "Sounds simplistic, but many of my friends have burned and crashed by torching the candle at both ends."

While all of these steps are important to a balanced and healthy life, the fact is that for some folks, the work itself is the best therapy. Rather than causing stress, the work provides a refuge from life.

I have always loved to draw and paint. There is nothing more satisfying than sitting down and getting into the "zone." The zone is quite addicting. My mind focuses only on what I am doing for that very moment, concentrating on every pencil or brush stroke. Everything else around me falls into the far background. Time just fades away, sometimes for hours on end.

It's a funny thing: I am usually very relaxed after a painting or drawing session. Or I am quite energized. But either way, I am rather ecstatic and incredibly content.

REAL-WORLD ALERT

Your exercise regime, hobbies, and relaxation methods may be far different from mine. What I know is that the balance of work to play rounds off the edges of stress and hyperactivity. What I understand is that eating right and regular (plus getting the sleep to back it up) gives me the endurance to sustain the juggling act.

But I am far, far from perfect in the life–maintenance department. Don't get me wrong—the agenda makes good sense, and I strive to practice what I preach. Generally, the machine hums pretty smoothly.

But I blow it. All the time. And so will you. However, I have doped out the secret to keeping the program going for the long haul: forgiveness.

I'm not talking about rationalization (although, as Jeff Goldblum's character in The Big Chill says, see if you can go a whole day without one rationalization). I try hard not to beat myself up when I fail (at least, not too much—brute-force guilt in small doses is sometimes an effective motivator).

I had a major speaking engagement go sour on me a few years back. Truth is, it was the audience evaluations that didn't pan out. I didn't flop; immediate feedback was actually wonderful—it was a bit like being a rock star. However, I eventually learned that I didn't go over with a chunky percentage of the written respondents.

When I got this news, I gave myself permission to feel the whole gamut of emotions, positive and negative. I was disappointed and discouraged. But I also lived in the sweet spot of a certifiably fun gig. I acknowledged that I pulled off a major coup (the heady experience of speaking to a crowd of 500-plus colleagues). Honestly, the sheer fact that I had really pulled that off—and that I didn't soil my trousers—was worth the bad reviews alone. And then I admitted that I wasn't universally loved. This was humbling for a chronically people-pleasing, habitual nice guy.

And I survived *that*. I've gone on to other (successful) speaking appearances since. So I can give you my own best advice: When you stumble or hit a pothole, own up, *but own it 100 percent*: the good, the bad, and the ugly.

Give yourself the leeway to gloriously wallow in all of the muck for a brief spell (the rock-star and the rock-pile stuff), and do remind yourself to be kind to the most important cog in the wheel: *you*. Then clean up and move on.

Staying with It

As important as it is to have friends and interests outside of illustration, it is just as important to keep your involvement within the field of illustration alive and current. "You must remember that illustration, to some extent, is a business, and what you create is a product," Spollen reflects. "This does not in any way diminish your work."

And it's the work that sparks the passion, after all. How does Spollen maintain his interest, that creative enthusiasm we mentioned earlier?

"Get lots of visual stimulation (aka eye candy) in your life. All kinds of books and magazines. A few I recommend are *Juxtapoz*, *3x3*, the *Communication Arts* Illustration Annual, and, of course, the Society of Illustrators (NY) Annual.

"Visit the Society of Illustrators Web site for weekly events, shows, and updates. Join your local art group or illustrators' club. Make it a habit to go to your nearest museum. Attend art shows."

And here Spollen puts a wise spin on the concept of recharging your batteries. "This may sound strange," he begins, "but at a certain point in your career it helps to stand back and reevaluate your work.

"Try to remember what it was that made you want to create in the first place. Go back and explore those images from your past that you enjoyed so very much when you were young. Colors, events, sounds—whatever it was that took your breath away and filled you with the desire to create. It's cheap and it's easy and it's a fun way to reboot your magic."

Spollen is saying it is wise to know your history, to appreciate "where you came from." The old spark is still right there—just bring it back into focus.

"I always liked boats, planes, and hot rods—images that I still feel very passionate about," Spollen says, illustrating his point. "Now I am revisiting these friendly images with my new work, titled *Surf Beach*. I must also admit that I crank up 'Please Please Me,' a favorite Beatle tune, as this work is created; the music adds to the joy of the creative flow."

DAGOODOLDAZE

Revisiting old journals and sketchbooks is one of the ways Winn–Lederer maintains her creativity. "I often find old ideas or fragments of ideas worth developing *now*. In fact, I occasionally add comments to past thoughts/observations and date them accordingly. "Another technique is to browse through my personal library," she adds, "choose a book at random, and open it to a random page. Often a word or phrase will be enough to trigger the creative juices."

"I can tell you the very first time I truly captured my subject on paper," Erin Brady Worsham remembers. "I was fourteen and I stayed up all night drawing a picture of David Bowie and coloring it with oil pastels.

"At 7 A.M., I finished and looked into the recognizable face of Ziggy Stardust. I was so ecstatic, I couldn't resist running barefoot through the

summer-dew-laden grass to my friend's house across the street to show her my masterpiece. I never want to lose that wonder."

"For me, it is a natural flow most of the time," Jenny Kostecki-Shaw says. "However, there are challenging times when I have to actively find that passion—a connection.

"What works for me consistently is to incorporate something personal—the retro orange rotary phone or the coffee-percolator lamp in my studio. Or I reach for my travel journals, sketchbooks, and my memory and incorporate something fun—a unique pattern or color palette or a doodle from a coffee shop or the zoo—whatever relates—into my job."

Face the work you have to do today by tapping into a most important resource: you (and your history). Same thing with having daydreams. Certainly think ahead, envision a bigger success, a better tomorrow. But, of course, to manifest this future, you should take action *today*—you must live and work in the here and now.

A KICK IN THE RIGHT PLACE

Following this train of thought, deadlines can also become distilled motivation. The clock or calendar often generates inspiration in its purest, crystalline form. "If I am honest with myself," Ken Meyer, Jr., says, "I know that deadlines, whether self-imposed or from another source, keep me going and producing."

Meyer also points out that that many of us luxuriating with a long deadline *still* wait until the last minute to get the job done. "That sets us up to fail, though. Invariably, just when you're ready to work on that piece you are finally getting around to, another equally important job comes in with the same deadline. You're screwed, basically," he says frankly.

"You will face these situations," Meyer continues. "Jobs you need to accomplish in a day or a week, or even a few hours. Jobs that force you to put aside other tasks. Recently, I got an e-mail on a Saturday morning from an art director who saw my work on an online portfolio site (I had just signed up for it the previous day, amazingly enough).

"He needed a full-blown King Kong illustration by Monday . . . Kong on a building, planes, spotlight, the whole bit. The pay was good; I just could not refuse (and didn't want to, this being a possibly good contact for future work).

© Ken Meyer, Jr.

"If you can turn in good work on a short deadline like this, it shows you're a hard worker, adaptable, dependable. You can be their go-to guy. And, hopefully, get jobs with longer deadlines in the future as well!"

Swim or Die

Says Scott Bakal: "A routine is key in trying to build an illustration business."

"Keep drawing and keep creating pictures. If there is no work coming in, go out and paint that series of visuals you've been thinking about for months. When you're finished with this work, you may have something marketable in itself—the beginning of a graphic novel, children's book, print series, or even just portfolio pieces. Having a routine for creating will keep you in the game of creating."

Much like a shark who must keep moving to live, Bakal recommends maintaining a schedule to sketch, draw, or paint, even during slow times. "You must keep working or you will lose your creative momentum," he counsels, "and eventually you may stop creating all together. That would be the biggest shame of all."

Learn and Grow

"As I continue to progress—hopefully for the better—I just go with my instincts," Scott Jarrard comments. "I do what I feel is the right thing to do and do what I think looks good."

What feels right will look good. Repeat that wonderful mantra; these are true words to live by. Erin Brady Worsham was once asked to do a memorial portrait, a final illustration of the subject's life. "Portraits have never been my thing," she says, "and the assignment was further complicated by the fact that the woman—whose job it was to plan large social functions—had taken her own life.

"I didn't feel it would be appropriate to depict her in the present day, because that had obviously been painful for her. Instead, I painted her welcoming the viewer to a large, outdoor, Brueghel-esque gathering. It was festive and full of life. The client was happy and I felt like I had captured something of her spirit."

"Living in the here and now also means learning new things," Jarrard says. "I try to learn new technologies and techniques. This keeps me living today and not in the past."

More great advice: *Keep it fresh to stay vital.* "For me, it's calligraphy," Ward Schumaker says. "People hire me to do portraits, for instance, and up the pay by having me add a calligraphic quote beneath.

"My wife, Vivienne Flesher, has added photography as an adjunct to her illustration work. Not only did Vivienne start taking pictures, but she's also sold her first book of photographs (of her dog), called *Alfred's Nose.*

"We've also been getting a few jobs together," Schumaker tells us. "*SEE* Magazine (published by furniture maker Herman Miller) hired Vivienne to do a series of portraits, and me to do a spread for the same article.

"*American Illustration* had us do a spread together—Vivienne did a nude, I superimposed my cut out paper lettering. And this weekend we're both working for the same art director at the *Los Angeles Times Book Review* for the same edition."

Fact-of-Life Department: Change is inevitable and inescapable. You have ten seconds to comply. Resistance is futile, silly human. Why fight it?

Taking chances is scary. But breaking new ground can stimulate you immensely. You can *make* that stretch—you *can* reach higher. Often exactly what we need or want is out on that limb.

As Jarrard says, "Every time I get out of my comfort zone and take on a project that is out of my normal routine, I stress. But nine times out of ten, my client will love it—and once I have heard that they're happy, I'll be happy."

This I understand all too well. In my early days of exploring digital illustration, I took on a big job that required me to work in Adobe Illustrator. I was more of a raster kinda guy back then, but the project promised to be a great gig on many levels, so I felt that I couldn't turn it down. I thought I could do it (and should do it), but there was one little pesky detail: I had to learn *how*.

I was way out of my comfort zone, and I can still clearly recall the high anxiety that hit me the moment after I made the written commitment. I knew Photoshop somewhat but had to actually learn Illustrator and figure out a whole new routine.

My system was decent, but not the hot rod I truly needed. I was constantly doping out workarounds to compensate for low RAM and punk processing power (I crashed constantly but made sure I never crashed and burned). I had to rent a photocopier and buy some hardware, software, and other necessities—just to get started. Plus I had to duck out of a little family vacation to meet the initial deadline. Why was I doing this again?

Because my inclinations were absolutely correct. The assignment *was* a hoot—wow, was it fun (especially playing with the photocopier). The money, even after allowing for my buying spree and learning curve, was quite okay. My satisfied client asked me to do more work.

I learned a wonderful new application that became (and remains) my program of choice. I grew creatively and, in retrospect, my illustration simply took off from here. I figured out invaluable work patterns that serve me to this day. My career as a computer tech (maybe that's actually spelled "geek") began with this job, too.

But had I succumbed to the panic and stress of the situation—the "stay put; you're much safer" mode—it would be a different story. Change oozes growth potential. There are always outcomes with change. No guarantees of pain-free results, of course, but *results* are always worth effort and risk.

"And change is what our art/illustration world is currently all about," adds Spollen matter-of-factly. "Don't be afraid of change—embrace it. Which is easier said than done, of course," he adds with a wink.

Tom Graham has a scenario for you. "Illustration in books and period-icals has declined," he begins. "Fees for what work there is have dropped. The economics of publishing have changed; production costs force publishers to save money where they can.

"Magazines have gone out of business. There's intense, increased com-petition from new media. Tastes change. Society is changed by war."

Sound familiar? As you're nodding in agreement, understand that Graham's not reading from the latest Graphic Artists Guild newsletter. He's referring to the late 1920s through the 1930s in America.

Balance

The fundamental goal for all of us should be to establish and maintain the mix of skills as well as the sense of personal (and professional) perspective we need to balance a life as an illustrator.

This idea of proportion—that life must be vital at and away from the drawing board—is how a busy professional maintains *business as usual*, sustaining himself as well as home and family.

7

The Field

What would I do if I didn't do this job?
Frankly, I don't know what else.

—ISABELLE DERVAUX, ILLUSTRATOR

How You Fit   In general, what and where is the illustrator's place in the professional world? We'll explore the question in two parts. First, we'll discuss some market opportunities (the various arenas that make up the field itself: advertising and editorial, animation, manufactured products like clothes and toys, the Web, etc.). Then we'll examine the illustrator's role, issues that impact the job, and hot-button topics that affect the illustrator's professional niche: "avant-garde" versus "conventional" illustration; dealing with competition; artistic integrity, creative control, and originality.

Let's Book

Indeed. Solving graphic problems is what being an illustrator is all about, what many might say is exactly your professional place in the world.

© Rick Sealock

The book market is one such rich and rewarding arena in which to practice the craft of problem-solving.

Illustrators will create jackets and covers as well as inside pages. You'll work on activities (coloring books) and educational aids (flash cards), games and posters, advertising and promotion, communications and catalogs, plus point-of-purchase displays.

Maybe you are doing textbooks and educational materials. It could be scholarly works or professional titles. Perhaps special-interest books are your thing: instructional manuals, biographies. Don't forget fiction, cookbooks, and a particularly huge market: juveniles.

JUST KIDS' STUFF

"The good thing about working for the children's market is that you know *nothing can replace illustration*," Lizzy Rockwell will tell you. "Children learn about the world visually. Photography and graphics simply can't communicate

all the things that a child can learn from a picture. Illustrated images have the most versatility, timelessness, and psychological power. I really can't see being replaced by a machine.

"And I think this distinguishes the illustrator from the fine artist. I want my viewer to be pleased, to identify with the image, to learn something. I love doing work that is useful.

"But I think adults deserve this as well. In fact, I'm bracing for a renaissance of illustration and hand lettering any day now. Well, I can hope anyway!"

BOOK ENDS

That renaissance may be here already, precipitated by sheer diversity and direct necessity. One case in point: Matt McElligott. McElligott began his career as a freelance illustrator, eventually getting his first children's book published. "I got insanely lucky and landed a publisher the first place I sent it," he says. Later books did not come about quite so smoothly.

But patience and dedication paid off. More books followed (and the lag time diminished). However, he cautions, "What I had to understand was that being an author and promoting the book is a whole other job, in addition to actually writing and drawing it." He then started teaching full time. "It meant that it wasn't as big a financial requirement to keep doing the freelance illustration," he says. "I now had a steady paycheck.

"Plus, I just didn't have the time for it. Something had to go. And that was the freelance stuff. As I started to get more books, the other opportunities opened up—speaking engagements and things like that. I find that those now consume all the available time I have. So one thing sort of evolved into another.

"As much as I like illustration, I'm not sure I'm cut out to be a full-time illustrator. I think I'm somebody who needs variety, and teaching gives me that. I can come in and spend a couple of days in the classroom, I can spend other days drawing, or I can mix that up.

"I have only admiration for illustrators who have their style and can stick with it—really make that work five days a week or more. I'm not sure I can do that. Some of this came out of recognizing that that was the way I was wired."

And just a word here. Recognizing what you want to do doesn't always mean that you *can* do it. It may not be financially viable or you may not have the time to go in that direction. Ease into your path slowly and deliberately—with thought and preparation.

"Each year my direction changed, " McElligott will say. "But I didn't stop the freelance illustration cold turkey. It just sort of phased out as other things came into the picture."

Advertising Agencies/Design Studios

While McElligott specializes in book illustration, and no longer free-lances per se, the "other things" he alludes to are still vital stops in the illustration marketplace.

Working with advertising agencies and design studios will certainly be such an opportunity. You could be hired full time at such places (large or small), but chances are better you'll be signed as a designer who can illustrate, as opposed to being the staff illustrator.

In all likelihood, as an illustrator you'll be freelancing for these folks. And we should also say that while a pocket of dedicated illustration studios still exists, the salad days of such groups are past.

Ad agencies and design studios solve marketing problems for clients by developing copy and appropriate graphics for ads in magazines and newspapers; they produce radio and television commercials; conceive billboards and direct-mail campaigns; create interactive, multimedia, and Web sites; and produce literature, sales brochures, and other such collateral material.

You'll find some of these shops doing market research and public relations, as well. In a related arena, you may find yourself working for a public relations firm, often a direct network to ad agencies or design studios.

Greetings and Occasions Market

If you like keeping your eyes on popular culture, the greetings/occasions market is a good fit for your illustration. Cards reflect contemporary subject matter and topics of special interest to the card buyer. Current trends and changing lifestyles of consumers (as well as traditional themes and holidays) dictate a steady need for product.

Both freelance and full-time opportunities exist in a market always on the lookout for bright ideas and innovative styles. Licensing opportunities are a potentially lucrative option for entrepreneurs (check out the exploding vinyl toy market as proof positive here).

Freelancing: a world of no guarantees and never knowing what tomorrow might bring. As a result, you tend to become very prudent, which actually establishes a certain sanctuary. It's crazy—as a freelance illustrator, I was so unsure of myself that I spent most of my time working to make my little world secure (all the while searching for that quiet space to create).

—CHRIS SPOLLEN, ILLUSTRATOR

In the greetings and occasions industry, a design is essentially the same as an illustration; the term "design" referring to the visual element that accompanies the editorial (the copy) on a card.

Techniques are wide open. Stylistically, almost anything goes. Any medium can be used for a design. Your art may be used for a single purpose— a select card, one page, or an individual spread in a booklet or calendar. Or you may be doing a series of cards, or a multicomponent campaign of cards and related products (cards, calendar, mugs, apparel, etc.).

Along those lines, the company may produce related paper products (note cards, stationery, party goods, and gift wrap) or an electronic product line (e-cards, for instance).

Magazines

Traditionally, doing editorial work for the magazines market was step one for illustrators. By a long shot, the magazine market is not what it used to be, but this venue is still a good place to work.

This changing (and these days challenged) market remains wide open and diverse. Look for local and regional publications, trade journals, general audience or consumer periodicals, special—interest magazines, and in—house or company publications.

Obviously, publications are directed to specific readers. Every magazine has its own editorial (and visual) flavor. Copy, photography, and illustration share the pages of any periodical. Magazines look for illustrators who can do four—color or black—and—white art, doing both digital and traditional illustration.

The Internet

Unless you've lived underground for the last two decades, you know that it's imperative to have a Web site (and now, a blog). Used to be, marketing and promotion meant mailers and pages in the creative directories; phone calls plus portfolio drop—offs and reviews. But thanks to the digital revolution and the Internet, all aspects of the illustration business are very different now; the brave new world is here.

The computer has dramatically and dynamically changed art production and delivery. The rise of the Internet has created unparalleled *global* business, marketing, and promotional opportunities for illustrators. Electronic communications have created a international village of artists, time zones (even language barriers) be damned. Connections have never been better; networking has never been easier or as efficient.

On Edge

What does "cutting edge" mean? What is the cutting edge of illustration these days? To be viable, must you work out on that edge?

Edge. Now, that's a word that gets bandied about all the time. So, what *is* this "edge" thing? One always hears about "edgy" art. This fabled "cutting edge" has been honed for some time, it seems.

How sharp is the cutting edge? And how'd it get so sharp? And while we're at it, who's this "avant-garde" we're always hearing about? Hey, are the avant-garde keen on this cutting edge?

PO-*TAY*-TO, PO-*TAH*-TO

Before we make any determinations, let's consider our cultural perception of "cutting edge" as opposed to what's considered "conventional." So here's a good first question to ponder: Is what was edgy ten years ago still edgy today?

In the later nineteenth century, the wonderful (and influential) Franklin Booth taught himself to draw by studying pictures from the available publications of his day. He meticulously explored and crafted his exquisitely chiseled line quality from what he mistakenly thought to be state-of-the-art reference, never realizing that his resources were actually steel or wood engravings, and not pen and ink drawings at all. He was cutting edge by accident!

In the 1920s, the "Ashcan School" of art was considered edgy. The "ashcan" appellation was not complimentary, but the derisively labeled group was ultimately and extremely important. Also called "the Eight," its center was painter/teacher Robert Henri, and this maverick organization of painters boasted illustrators like William Glackens, Everett Shinn, and John Sloan.

"I find it highly ironic that the Eight—many of them illustrators from Philadelphia, by the way—helped sow the seeds of their own stylistic demise," illustrator (and illustration historian) Tom Graham points out. "By helping to organize the Armory show in 1913, they introduced many modernist painters (and avant-garde ideas about art) from Europe to the US."

In the 1950s, creative innovation was certainly the new order (put another way—the cutting edge). An idea called "conceptual illustration" was a revolutionary direction for illustration. The rise of conceptual illustration saw illustrators playing with abstract (as well as representational) expressionism. This generation's illustrators loved wit and satire. Modern, primitive, and comic art was all fair game; they played with metaphor and symbolism (rejected by their predecessors, but embraced as the cutting edge this time around).

"The fifties," Graham tells us, "introduced conceptual solutions, but, logically enough, also saw the breakdown of the absolute requirement to draw traditionally—in a representational manner. Realism gave way to pluralism (many styles coexisting). Still true today."

The 1980s were labeled years of "New Illustration." That sure sounds cutting edge to me. But from this vantage point, a careful look at process and product through the decades reveals that all eras have "New Illustrators."

Don't get me wrong. At this writing, in our era, there's plenty of creative juice and technochievements to go around (and yes, I just coined that word). Free and forward thinking? I think we have that one covered, too. We live in a remarkable time.

My read of history simply shows me that all periods boast rebels and innovators whose entrepreneurial attitude, grand concepts, and virtuoso technique fly against what was then the establishment.

For example, Norman Rockwell's influence was huge. He was once the new kid on the (watercolor) block, then a top dog for decades, and eventually considered conventional and safe, if not stale.

Here's a thought: "New Illustrators" go on to eventually *become the establishment*, and another crew of upstarts reject, rethink, and reshape the status quo. Like Elvis, the old guard never really leaves the building. Staying power is one thing, but you start to hear words like "retro," "homage," and soon, "parody." Like old clothes, old style seems to come back into style eventually.

A Rose by Any Other Name

Well, then, is it important to at least fit in? By classical definition (and/or perception), aren't artists *expected* to be "different"?

"Titles are just so silly," says PJ Loughran. "It's a way for people to categorize, to simplify, to make sense of somebody (or their work). I try to avoid that stuff as much as I can."

"It used to be the standard to be original and *different* in creating your unique illustrations," Rick Sealock laments. "Now it's called 'quirky' because it may not be as commercially viable and tolerated as before.

"But these folks were always the most interesting to *me*," he says. "Usually never boring and always original thinkers. Illustrators are supposed to be thinkers, challenging and pushing cultural boundaries and thus educating the public. The imposed 'political correctness' and corporate philosophies of our society created this adverse label in an attempt to curb this originality."

There is that school of thought that rails against any or all conformity—the idea that if you "fit in," you'll actually lose the (creative) edge. Personal or professional compromise may be real or imagined, but, according to Sealock, artistic integrity must be maintained.

© Tom Graham

"It seems there is so much suck illustration being created. And more than ever, it will dumb down the industry," Sealock cautions.

Hmm . . . any *alternatives* to all this?

Alternative Realities

When one is described as "alternative," what is meant by that? Alternative to what? Aren't artists in general an alternative to "regular" folks? Is there a perception/reality conundrum involved with this label?

And then there is the other side of the coin—when one is described as being "part of the establishment," what do we mean here? What *is* the establishment, and is this a positive or a negative?

"I'm progressive," Paul Melia says. "I am with the times or ahead. But I wouldn't consider myself cutting edge—that's not me. And those are just words. They don't bother me. I do what's inside of me. If someone accepts it or pays me for it, or has a positive reaction, I'm lucky.

"But I don't pay much attention to that stuff. You know, some stuff done in the so–called 'modern age' is crap, some of it is really good. But you can't worry about the labels, you simply must do what you do. You let the chips fall where they may.

"No matter what anybody says about my work, I can only be what I am. I can't force it. Oh, I'd love to think of myself as an avant–garde artist, but I'm not—I just do what I love to do."

Establishment

A question: When you're part of the "establishment," what exactly are you establishing? It may actually be a roots thing—tradition. And while artists may be considered (or consider themselves) to be outsiders, when enough

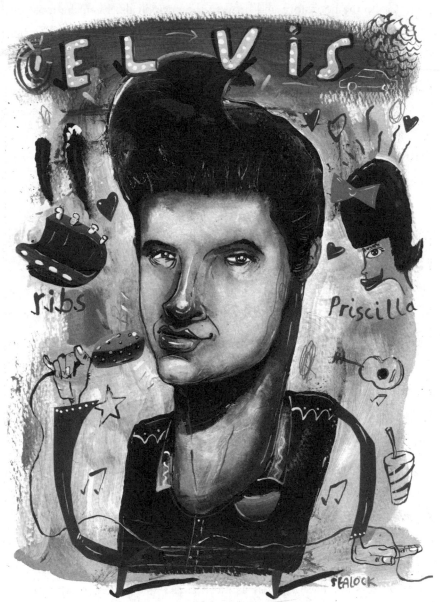

outsiders band together, they become a club, or even a movement of their own. Go to the bookstore and browse the periodicals. Even the most off-center lifestyles and/or practices have magazines (and Web sites, these days) dedicated to that culture. These devotees sum up an "establishment," as I see it.

"There are those illustrators who go wild and crazy on the page because it is the acceptable thing at the moment," Greg Nemec points out. "Their illustration has an avant-garde hook to it, but it's whatever is hip *at the moment*—'Hey, look at me, I'm edgy.' That seems pretty establishment to me."

"I'm not what I would call part of the establishment or mainstream," Melia continues. "And as far as an 'establishment' is concerned, it exists in any established arena—applied arts, creative arts, even government, whatever.

"You might have to deal with it, play the game, certainly pay attention to it. I do what *I* do as honestly as I can do it. I don't let the tags influence me too terribly. I just don't think about it that much."

"My illustration work is fairly realistic," illustrator Derek Brazell tells us. Brazell, a British illustrator specializing in children's books, says his work is thus perceived as not particularly *contemporary*. "I think my style *is* current, but work in this vein is not addressed at conferences or in magazine articles.

"Sometimes it's frustrating that editorial work gets all the glory," he says. "Many working illustrators are nowhere near the 'cutting edge' but do supply a huge amount of illustration for educational, informational, and children's markets. And often, I believe, those who talk about what illustration 'should' be are academics or practitioners who don't make their living producing images that they consider as mere 'bread-and-butter' work.

"Like actors, it's easy for us to be pigeonholed," Brazell cautions. "And it can happen so gradually that you don't notice for years. If you're happy with that, then it's fine, but it can be a struggle to break free."

WHERE IS THE MIDDLE OF THE ROAD?

Can you get anywhere in the middle of the road? Sure you can. I'll play devil's advocate for the Artmobile Association of America (completely fictional, by the way) and ask, Isn't the middle of the road a line to somewhere?

Yes, it is the safer path (as opposed to driving on the edges—a much bumpier ride). It's your say; anything anyone else tells you is a judgment call. Neil Young, when discussing his record *Harvest*, said he found himself heading squarely down the middle of the road with this album. He saw that he was being very successful doing this, but that it wasn't where he really wanted to be traveling. Yet—at least from my point of view—he returns to this genre again and again. What's the road map here, then?

"I feel like I'm more of the middle of the road," Ali Douglass muses. "The 'average guy' appreciates my work, but a 'hip chick' may look at a piece and possibly laugh—it's too 'happy and cute.' But *I'm* excited about it, and it's all good to me."

Competition

Who's traveling with you down the middle of that road (or racing against you, to your left or right)? Your competition, of course.

I'm not sure competition is either a "good" or a "bad" thing. I believe the filter is attitude: simple motivation and drive, how *you* handle the competition.

It's not about who (or what) the competition may be. Nor is it a grudge match between fact and fiction—real competition and imagined competition.

"All illustrators are competitors," says Sealock, "sometimes with others and always with themselves. We compete with every illustration we have created and the ones we want to create.

"We compete with our skill level/technical ability. We compete with our preexisting concepts, our notions, and our expected approaches. We compete against labels and definitions, fears and security. We compete!"

MAKING IT

In the best of all possible worlds, illustrators would handle competition by focusing on the true heart of the matter: the art. Nothing else would matter. That's a sweet dream, and if it's yours (like it is mine), never lose it. But for some illustrators, specific benchmarks of success stoke their competitive fires. Recognition. Awards. Status. A certain salary.

"Is this the devil's-advocate part of the book?" Sealock asks. "It's more the business of creating illustrations than selling illustration. For me, the creativity portion is separate from the price tag.

"I create images I love and need to and it's a bonus that someone wants them and will pay for them. Again, each to his own. If you decide to judge the creative level by its dollar value, then fine—that's your decision. It's just not mine."

For some, the criteria is just doing their personal best. "I think most people like to be known by others, to be appreciated, admired perhaps," comments Ken Meyer, Jr. "My goal for many years has been to get into the Society of Illustrators Annual. When I do that, I will feel I have 'made it.' Although I have an equal feeling that if I do, I will just feel good and move on."

There are illustrators who just don't spend much time worrying one way or another. "Many people work in a similar style," reflects Greg Nemec, "but I really don't think about it much."

Some illustrators are able to compete without acknowledging that it's a competition; they simply choose to blissfully ignore. There are those who *refuse* to compete—although if you disregard the competition, or choose not to compete, you will want to consider what that means for you and for your business growth. Freelance illustrators are in the business of selling illustration; competition is a powerful sales motivation.

Sell Sell Sell

As long as we're discussing sales, let me say that selling your illustration doesn't mean you are selling out.

"*Giving it away* is losing your integrity!" Sealock states emphatically. Yes, there are artists—who shall remain nameless—who have sold out and done quite well for themselves. If this was a fiction, the label "sellout" would be a nonsense phrase.

And yes, folks with little (or no) artistic integrity have, nonetheless, become tremendously successful. Poster children for soulless greed? Oh, I don't know if we'll go that far here. Nor will we get that worked up about it (at least in these pages), and mainly because, as Sealock says artistic integrity is, "Whatever you think is correct for you."

He's right; morals and ethics are a personal choice. And as my friend Roger Brucker says, "There's no right way to do the wrong thing."

"Personally, money comes and goes," Sealock continues, "but your integrity has to remain intact, defended to the end. It's difficult to do at times, as we're only human, but you must try—and that is the key.

"Giving it away for free *would* be a compromise, and if you feel it's really worth nothing, then give it away. But if you feel it is worth something, then get something for it."

Originality

It's not hard to find illustration (especially on the Internet) that's blatantly tasteless or politically questionable (even reprehensible). It's a big world of free speech; I'll bet you know illustrators who dabble in this stuff (I do).

But I don't personally know illustrators whom I consider unethical. I'm not professionally aware of any colleagues doing anything illegal with their art. However, the issues of originality get a bit stickier.

Have you ever admired another artist's work to the degree that your work starts to look like his?

Let's consider what constitutes a "rip-off," the point when emulation (or imitation) become plagiarism. When is all—or any—of this too close for comfort?

It is hard to argue that an overtly blatant swipe is only a simple or mis-guided mistake. But in that we all are the product of our inspirations and influ-ences, truly *original* illustration is much akin to the holy grail—realistically, we are the byproduct of our adaptation and adoption.

Can you fully divorce your mind's eye from reference and resources? I hear the expression "Good artists borrow, great artists steal" on a semireg-ular basis. What do we make of this sly and oft-used adage?

Illustrator Jason Greenberg puts it this way: "If I'm understanding it correctly, 'they're' actually saying, 'Good artists oftentimes are trendy, but great artists innovate.'

"But it's all about being *original* in this world. Be aware of your sur-roundings; but there is no need to steal or even borrow from that context. There are way too many clones running around trying to fit into the lump. Find something you can offer, get in touch with who *you* are; otherwise, you'll end up a second-rate hack, a module."

Okay. You just might debate that the quote is not about innovation but is all about appropriation. You might argue more strenuously that it's actually about adaptation. And depending on your interpretation of the adage, you may not buy it to any degree—which is fine—but I hope it makes you go a little deeper on the subject.

Here's another take: "Good artists borrow, great artists steal?" Julia Minamata asks. "I've got to tell you, I've never really understood that saying. I don't know what the original meaning was, but I interpret it like this: 'Steal' something, keep it, and make it your own.

"A great artist takes something she likes (say, a certain color palette or a line quality), and through her own self-expression, transforms it into something that is unique to her; she owns it."

Yep. I get that. Let me refer you back to illustrator Franklin Booth, who thought he was emulating the style of his day but came up with a trademark (and original) technique.

© Julia Minamata

"One of the great things about being an illustrator is that there is so much potential for self-expression," Minamata continues. "We're all inspired by tons of things, but the trick is to take what you like and make it personal and unique.

"People who emulate/imitate a popular, trendy style (or artist) are lazy and selling themselves short. We're all distinctive and different—the ultimate goal is to be successful and happy being who you are, not pretending to be someone else.

"Now, wouldn't that make you happier? Be yourself! Find clients who like you for who you are. It might be harder, but ultimately it is far more rewarding."

CONTROL ISSUES

And directly related to all the topics we're discussing is another hot-button issue for illustrators: artistic control. In a nutshell: You don't have to give it up. On the contrary.

But here's another nutshell: You must exploit creative opportunities and work hard to make such artistic control a reality. That means establishing a solid reputation (backed by the strong portfolio of work that built that rep). You get and/or keep artistic control by doing stellar illustration and establishing clean, clear communications with art buyers and art directors. And, of course, coming through.

If the integrity of your art is a concern (and it should be), learn the power of one word: *no*. "No" means not taking a job if it's not right for you. "No" means you only agree to terms you can accept. "No" means never signing a deal unless you know exactly what the job will entail on all fronts: requirements, expectations, specs, calendar, and deadlines.

You can still smack into the ugly end of the beast, but reasonably wielding the power of this simple word can make your life much, much easier.

Win. Place. Show.

So what is the illustrator's place in the professional world? Here we took a look at what's out there in the marketplace and how artists find their place in it. My bet is you'll examine these concerns daily as you entertain creative opportunities (that illustration on your drawing board) via the opportunities to create (the world of illustration).

8

Marketing and Promotion

I like stability and I love pleasing clients. I'm in the business of selling my talent to the highest and nicest bidder. Aren't we all?

—JAY MONTGOMERY,
 ILLUSTRATOR AND EDUCATOR

Bad for Business   An illustrator's career is a bit like juggling *and* solving a jigsaw puzzle simultaneously. Keeping all the elements—creative techniques and process, business systems and procedures, info (records and files) and calendar (deadlines and schedule)—up in the air while you put all the pieces together to make the art. One crucial component in this mix will be bringing in clients. And to do that, you need to market and promote.

It's generally considered true that creative folks, including illustrators, are "bad" (or, at best, reluctant) businesspeople. Many artists shudder at the very idea of being a "salesperson." We immediately imagine we're hawking snake oil to bumpkins, or palming off aluminum siding on unsuspecting retirees.

Do *you* feel that way?

Buying and Selling the Process

As Jay Montgomery will tell you, marketing graphic arts is unlike plumbing and selling cars, but similar rules apply to all selling. "I've been an image problem–solver for over twelve years," he says. "I have come to realize that if you want to do art to please yourself, show your own vision and aesthetics and become a 'fine artist.' By all means, please yourself.

"If you want to make a more stable living, then you have to create art the way other people want it," Montgomery goes on. "Hopefully you can get some joy out of that at the same time.

"Some fine artists doing illustration have a hard time giving in to the clients' needs and will only do it their way. That's fine for a few clients; most want the control they are paying for. I sell my services by promoting my work process (as seen from the clients' eyes) on my Web site. I explain it when negotiating, as well as writing it all out on an estimate. People buy process. They feel more comfortable knowing how the process will go, especially since all artists work differently. It's essential to educate your clients—and have the patience to do so. That's selling."

Sales Job

Sales—at least in the creativity biz—*is* marketing and promotion, and hardly below your calling. If you're in the business of selling your art and reject sales, you certainly need to have an attitude adjustment (unless you want your illustration *career* to tank).

"Illustration, by nature, is an entrepreneurial vocation," Sam Viviano says. "Most illustration is freelance; you work for yourself" (which is a classical definition of the term "entrepreneur").

"It's increasingly important to seek out your market," Viviano continues. "The commonly accepted markets for 'illustrators' are changing at a greater pace than ever before." Marketing and promotion is really art–speak for "How can I help you?" In this chapter, we'll discuss how a marketing and promotional program can help *you* find clients and help buyers recognize that you are their illustrator of choice, the artist who can solve that pesky graphics problem.

We'll begin with a general field guide and segue into a professional overview.

To Market

The first piece of the puzzle will be finding clients. Ask one simple question: "Who can use my services?" Ad agencies or design studios? General juvenile (and/or adult) product development and promotion? Book and magazine publishers? Greeting cards, toys, and games?

Consider *who* needs your illustration. *Why* are you the right guy for the job? Think about *where* your talents can best be applied. Evaluate *how* your skill level and illustration style match potential markets.

Look for potential business everywhere. Check out your options constantly. If you need a little push to start here, just go to the mall and window shop.

Networking

Networking is another component of marketing and promotion. The support system of your network can also yield referrals and leads, plus tangible inroads to markets. I heartily endorse organizations like the Graphic Artists Guild, the Illustrators' Partnership of America, your local art directors' club, the Society of Illustrators, and AIGA. And don't overlook peripheral professional groups affiliated with the communications field or other executive organizations.

The Range

Marketing and promotion take many forms. These days, a Web site is a must, and blogs are big, but illustrators still advertise their services on paper, plus contact clients via e-mail, phone and fax, and good ol' snail mail. The pendulum is definitely swinging electronically—it's easy, global, and immediate—but modern illustrators most likely promote with a combination of both digital and print.

Along with their Web site and/or blog, many illustrators join online portfolio groups and link to talent portals and photo-sharing Web sites (aka Web services or online communities).

Self-promotional mailers, capability brochures, and targeted direct mail are still part of the mix, as are the creative directories (which offer print and electronic options) and illustration competitions (and accompanying annuals). Actual portfolio drop-offs and reviews are somewhat of a trudge in recent times, but still possible.

Of course, illustrators still work with reps. Major metropolitan professional organizations and art institutions may offer local talent directories (print and/or electronic) as well. Pro bono services are one way to can get your name out there (for instance, design and/or illustrate the poster for a popular and prestigious fund-raising event).

Because of my eagerness to please any given client, my work tends to be all over the place in style and process. But there are, of course, some common threads throughout.
—JAY MONTGOMERY, ILLUSTRATOR AND EDUCATOR

Artists can advertise in the newspaper and list in the phone directories, too. Regional media advertising—television and radio—can be an interesting local opportunity (an announcement on your cable channel, perhaps). I would bet some artists still do cold calls! Whatever works.

Nurture *and* Nature

From years of field and classroom practice, Benton Mahan recognizes a proven work ethic that never "goes out of style"—a tried-and-true method to increase sales and pump production. "It varies from class to class, year to year," he says, "but the entrepreneurial spirit is alive and well in many of my students—these are serious folks *who know how to hustle.*

"When you run out of work, you become more creative," Mahan states from experience. And I know what he means. If the old markets aren't viable, *look for new ones*. Improve what's out there, or rethink it. Come up with a product (or service) and then market the hell out of it. It's about intensity, concentration, the aggressive pursuit of the prize. It's about sweat. "And truthfully, what else should you be doing with your time and gifts?" Mahan asks.

Niche markets, unexpected business opportunities, markets that didn't exist a few years back—all these supposedly peripheral venues—can be very lucrative. "A number of my students jump in before they graduate," Mahan will say. "Licensing is big. Internet comics. Character branding and product development. Online shops and convention sales. Web design. Speakers' gigs and self-publishing. Some illustrators are gravitating toward fine arts."

To Market We Will Go

Let's discuss these particular venues and how to market to each. Obviously you want to let your art speak for itself, but you'll want to tailor your promotion to a specific spot. "A promo should have its own personality. It's a display of your talent and of the good product you are selling; otherwise, the promotion will not deliver," illustrator Mike Quon advises.

If you don't have any professional, client-generated images to show, give yourself some assignments. Real jobs are important, and experience is not underrated. But self-confidence combined with strong art in a sample presentation can go far. Truth in advertising also works; you're looking for assignments, and everybody has to start somewhere. Have the credits read: "unpublished," or "personal work," or perhaps "portfolio piece." If the art is good (and fits a need for somebody), you won't be "unpublished" for long.

For the sake of this discussion, let's say you have a blog. So on your blog, display a two-page, full-color illustration that might complement a story you'd find in a magazine like *Spin*. Have five drawings that could be commissioned by *Sports Illustrated* for an article about the '57 Brooklyn Dodgers. Don't forget ten black–and–white spots a *New York Times* Op–Ed section may buy, and that *Juxtapoz*-style cover.

Create an illustrated roadmap of a two–week Tuscany vineyard tour that a reader might see in *Travel and Leisure* magazine. Develop characters for (and mock up) plush or vinyl toys. Create a line of alternative greeting cards. You could even send one card every two weeks to as many card companies as you can budget. Yep—a drive–by, serial mailing. Illustrate all the covers, as well as a few interior drawings, for a young–adult fantasy series.

Compile all your proudly rejected cartoons in an online gallery (even the ones that didn't make it into *The New Yorker*'s official reject collection). Boast up that fact—make it a badge of honor (which will further speak to your sense of humor). Self–publish and sell the volume of rejected cartoons through your Web site.

Develop characters (plus a product line) and work a booth at comics conventions or fantasy fairs. Give seminars at those same conventions. Run workshops at schools and clubs and for civic or private organizations (and always offer products to sell, as applicable).

Pitch book publishers. Self–publish. Go door to door electronically: Tap into the dynamic wave of online social networks (MySpace, Facebook, etc.) and image–sharing communities (Flickr, for instance) and get the word out there to all your new best friends.

IT'S ABOUT YOU

By the time Mahan's illustration students at the Columbus College of Art & Design are seniors, they have learned a lot about their direction in illustration. As it should be, each one explores style individually and, hopefully, discovers what is natural for him or her.

ABSOLUT®
Country of Sweden
VODKA

This superb vodka
was distilled from grain grown
in the rich fields of southern Sweden.
It has been produced at the famous
old distilleries near Åhus
in accordance with more than
400 years of Swedish tradition.
Vodka has been sold under the name
Absolut Since 1879.

ALC. 40%/VOL (80 PROOF)
PRODUCED AND BOTTLED IN SWEDEN
BY V&S VIN & SPRIT AB

IMPORTED

"Some students find that their talents lead them to children's illustration," Mahan says, "while others might go more painterly and more traditional. A few are design oriented. Conceptual. Comic book focused. Some are video game directed, or looking at Web animation (or cartoons), and so on.

"I ask my students to look at their own generation to help find markets for their talents. They are the future. Their interests—and the media they relate to—will be the markets of *their* time. I ask each student to make an honest evaluation of his natural talent (and direction) and develop and identify markets that are compatible for his illustration style.

"So I put a class together (at the Columbus College of Art & Design) that shifts a lot of the responsibility back to the students," Mahan tells us. "In this course, they must step up to the plate—just like in the real world— and research and figure out their marketplace (and how to fit into that marketplace).

"I felt strongly that students need some self-motivation when they graduate," he continues. "Classes are structured: Your roughs are due here, the final must be submitted there. But upon graduation, students will be out in the field, on their own. They will have to do it all, including the market research to get jobs."

Is this starting to sound familiar? "There are always folks who pursue a passion but are not sure they can make a living at it," Mahan goes on. "Maybe video games are your thing. In this class, you'll go find the companies that manufacture these games. You then must put together a portfolio to suit that market.

"I try to be realistic with my students: 'If you have trouble with drawing (or the computer, or whatever), this may not be the area you want to go into. But by the same token, if you want to *work hard* at it—go for it.'

"Many students just think about their art and not what they are going to do with it when they graduate. 'This is interesting,' I might comment, 'but what's the *market* for this?'

"You can't just hope that somebody is going to see the product and throw some work in your direction; I don't think life works that way. If anything, you need to get a Web site up and get postcards printed for a mailing (about five hundred, sent out a few times a year)."

In Mahan's class, students are required to organize a mailing list of fifty names; they have to mail out at least ten promo packages. These mailings consist of a cover letter, an 8.5" x 11" promo (with three illustration samples), plus a reply postcard (with room for comments and recommendations). And the kicker: Students must also land a real freelance job. Pay is not the issue; getting the assignment is.

Each illustration is accompanied by a mission statement—why they are doing the piece, how it fits into the marketplace. They are asked to justify why the art is a good portfolio piece. They must research the typical sale of rights, and pricing guidelines for a particular job. Then they draw up a contract and an invoice.

You might protest, "I don't go to CCAD; I'm not even in school!" You're wrong, you know—we're always in school, one way or another. You don't have to be in a formal academic setting to take advantage of Mahan's concept, you just have to put it in practice.

How do you write a mission statement? First, know your mission—what are you offering? To whom? Next, remember that the service you are selling is solving communications problems. So your mission statement is about goals: how this piece (or your style, concept, technique, philosophy—whatever) enhances the connection between artist and audience, client and buyer, author and reader.

A mission statement is a message of purpose: "I want this piece to say *this* about *that*. It's in my portfolio because it shows my particular strengths. You can apply that creative power to help you sell your widgets (in bulk, more efficiently, etc). Competitively, this service will cost you X amount of dollars (here you name a figure, perhaps, or talk generically about value). Here is the extent of my services (the rights) and what you get for your money. And reiterate: Here's why this is a bargain."

I like to write conversationally, so I suggest writing the mission statement (whether any client sees it or not) in user-friendly language that still makes a serious point. Get to the point with a minimum of fuss. But while casual is okay, don't forsake good writing mechanics (spelling and grammar).

RESEARCHING YOUR MARKETS

How do you research a particular market? As I said earlier, marketing and promotion takes many forms. The same methods you use to find markets are the same avenues the markets use to advertise.

Contact information has never been easier to dig up. Everybody and their proverbial mother has a Web site (and/or a blog) today, and it's not called the World Wide Web for nothing. I'm sure your mailbox is clogged with direct-mail advertising. Go to the library or bookstore, not just to research markets—browsing books, magazines, and newspapers—but to consult the directories of markets found in the reference section. Check out phone directories, watch TV, simply go online. And, of course, hit the mecca of market research—the mall.

Location

Is the old adage "Location is everything" correct? Must you live in a big city to have real success? Much of this depends on how your personal dictionary defines success (or "real," for that matter). "Success" is an elusive little bugger wherever you hang your shingle—big city or backwater burg. "It's all relative," all my relatives say, "but the subject is rather subjective."

Back in the day—oh, about or before 1984 B.D. (Before Digital)—I would've answered that question with a considered "certainly." Today, I would think that the answer is a qualified "no, not really."

We live in the age of the global community. Thanks to the Internet and the computer, you can effectively set up shop anywhere—you're only a few mouse clicks away from the heart, head, and wallets of the world.

Oh, sure, there's definitely more work in Metropolis than in Smallville (even Superman knew that), and service on the spot can still work to your advantage, but the challenges of time and distance have been seriously narrowed by that Mac in front of me and the cable line snaking behind my desk.

But this is just the means to the end, however. Energetic marketing and self-promotion, fueled by talent, elbow grease, and intensive customer service, is really what this chapter is all about.

"I don't know," muses Ali Douglass. "I don't think it really matters where I live. People find me a lot through the theispot (*www.theispot.com*)—a major illustration Internet site—or my Web site. I don't usually do portfolio drop-offs, and I rarely meet anyone I'm working with.

"It is all so *virtual*. I think it matters more that you're persistent with your own part of it: that you do the advertising and make the calls; that you *look* for work. Now, if I have a *local* job (here in San Francisco), people want to get together, which is interesting. It's not like that in New York, where they didn't care to meet me."

And here, Isabelle Dervaux joins the discussion. "These days, having a Web site is very direct—a portfolio review is instantaneous and international.

And yes, generally, it's hard to get appointments with art directors now to show your book. Art directors just aren't doing this anymore. They don't have *time* to see you. They'd rather check your work out on the Web or maybe look at print samples.

"But of course, you must continually update. And if you are marketing over the Web, you must pay attention to all the details, be very sales oriented, and stay on top of everything (the role a good rep plays, actually).

"I parted company with my U.S. rep, by the way, but still have reps in France and Japan. Even on the Web, I think it pays to have someone over there, due to time and cultural differences."

Selling

"Selling is not bullshit, it's problem-solving," Paul Melia declares emphatically. And Melia has successfully been in the game long enough to know. He's right, after all: Selling is solving *your client's* problem (not yours).

Is this all a polite euphemism for *selling out*? Doesn't feel that way to me—it's only self-awareness. If you're a good salesman, you must be *communicating*. Good communications provides options. Options mean knowing your job and striving to fill the job description.

"You're simply paying attention to what the real problem is, which ultimately reveals the right answer," Melia says. "If the client likes purple, you put in purple. *It's that easy*—and it takes veracity to do that.

"How to sell? Well, they must want your work to begin with," Melia says, "and is the customer always right? Let's just say, if they're paying for it, *of course*! To not do what the client wants (or asks for) can be counterproductive. The idea is to solve the problem—not become part of it."

CLEAR AS MUD

As said previously, you're in the communications business; think of yourself as a major player in the answers industry. That's quite a service indeed.

Good service is often equated with the notion of the "satisfied client." Illustrator Roger Brucker ran a marketing firm and is a bona fide marketing guru with decades of experience. He says, "Satisfied customers are not loyal; *delighted* customers are loyal. Wow customers by exceeding their expectations. [Give them] sacrificial service.

"In that service, as communicators," Brucker says, "we are paid to solve problems." Brucker says it is too easy to focus on the client and, ultimately, fail to understand the bigger picture (see below, as well as the sidebar, The Gospel [According to Brucker], on page 163.) After all, the message we're crafting to the customer is: clarity. Clarity is the most important goal.

"Our messages need to tell the customer how to solve his problem," Brucker continues. "How? By buying our product. Benefits, advantages, and features never go out of style. Too much crap is generated on the desire for cleverness rather than effective communication.

"If the message is persuasive, that's great. Bravo, if it's clever and creative. You may win an award in the art directors' show, but if the message is not clear, you may never get another assignment."

A GOOD PITCH

Do your clients know more about selling than you? What about this "customer is always right" thing? At the very beginning of the client relationship, Brucker tells a new client he is absolutely loyal to their marketing success.

Everything he recommends will be from that point of view. "If I tell them something they don't like," he says, "they need to remember that it is for the success of their business. And for this reason, I will speak my mind when I think something is not in their best interest.

"And I tell the whole chain of command the same story. This establishes a base for speaking truth with power.

"So the client says, 'We're having a whale of a sale. Let's show a great big whale in our new ad. My wife came up with that idea. Don't you think that's just terrific?'

Here, Brucker laughs and plays the value and clarity cards. "What do I say . . . 'Your wife is full of it, and she's ugly besides?' I would say: 'One of the easiest things to do in promotion is to use 'borrowed interest,' and the problem is that it is seldom effective (a lack of clarity) and it wastes your money (zero value).

'If you have unlimited money, we could do a whole series of whale ads. In this case we are trying to reach customers who want fine quality tools and a great selection at utterly fantastic clearance prices. We need to dramatize how wide the selection really is and how low the prices are.' Value and clarity.

"If the client still insists on the whale, I would tell them a story: *The Tale of the Young Illustrator*. Fresh out of art school, a young illustrator with a unique graphic style is offered an assignment. The client says, 'I want an illustration that looks just like Norman Rockwell; his *Saturday Evening Post* covers were so great! I'll pay you $5,000 for that illustration.'

"The young illustrator thinks: 'I don't want to do Norman Rockwell. That's dated, corny. People will flip the page, thinking they have seen the illustration before. I'll go back and tell my client just that.'

"Later, over coffee with an older artist buddy, the young illustrator discusses the meeting. He's crestfallen. 'What's wrong; how'd it go?' his colleague asks.

"'The client still wants Norman Rockwell.'

"'In that case, take a big basket back with you,' says the mentor. 'If some fool wants to throw $5,000 out the window, you need to be there to catch it.'"

Brucker's little fable isn't about selling out. It's about purpose. First of all, if the job really insults your artistic integrity (and you can't sway your client), *say no*. Walk. Yes—sigh—despite the money.

As the illustrator of record, you need to realize that your aesthetic creation is part of a larger message. It may be the emotional whammy that makes the words credible. Or it may be the clarifying visual that makes a complex message understandable. But it is *part* of the message, not the whole shebang.

"Illustrators who are merely 'decorators' are not going to get the lucrative jobs in the long run," Brucker comments. "Effective visual communicators will be in demand. Copywriters will love them, and so will art directors. The clients who pay the money and expect results will line up for their services."

GOAL!

A client with invisible expectations can burn your time and frustrate you. You must head off the mercurial client who says, "Just doodle up some stuff and I'll see how it hits me." Here Brucker generally asks (and right at the beginning), "What are we trying to accomplish here?"

"If the client is vague, I often will suggest something. It is easier for some customers to adjust what you propose than for them to pin down their own thinking. I once had a client who said, 'Roger, I want ads that really stop people, make them read the ad, and remember us.'

"When I returned with roughs that would accomplish that objective, the client said, 'No, no, no. These ads will not make my phone ring.'

"I realized that the client had shifted his objective and tried to blame me for working toward the 'wrong' goal. So in future work, I was always clear to say (again, right in the beginning), 'Now, we want people to stop and read the ad. We want them to remember the company, *and* we want the phone to ring, right?'"

The Gospel (According to Brucker)

Part 1:

The client says: "I want the viewer to understand exactly how this product works. So make me a front-view illustration that really shows off the cool design. It cost me ten big ones, and I'm really proud of it."

You say, "Rather than make an illustration of your product, how about we use a photo of the outside of the product? Then I can make a clear cutaway illustration of the inside to show the customer exactly how it works."

The customer comes back with, "But I only have the prototype. We won't have the production version until the trade show in one month. So a photo is out."

You say, "With Photoshop we can make the prototype look exactly like a photo of the production model, and the cutaway illustration will demonstrate that you have a superior design that works better than the competitor's product."

Part 2:

Illustrators serve a variety of markets, not all of them advertising. So here's a version of the above suitable for a magazine editor who wants a story illustration.

The editor says: "I want the viewer to visualize the climax of this story, where the hero talks the guy out of shooting himself with a gun. So make me a two-figure illustration that really dramatizes the crux moment when the hero reaches to take the gun."

You say, "I can make that illustration, but won't it tip off the outcome of the story at a glance? A reader might skip the story if he knows the gun will be handed over. How about we illustrate a gun with four hands on it. It will look like a struggle, but we won't know the outcome—we'll have to read the story!"

The customer comes back with, "Four hands on a gun? How can the reader possibly see it's a gun, let alone that there is a struggle going on?"

You say, "You're right—it will be tough to pull off, but I'm sure I can do it. Would you like to see a couple of roughs in three days? I think you'll be so pleased, you'll make it the lead story in that issue."

You Lucky Cluck

If you don't market and promote, your opportunities to create—at least for fun *and* profit—will be very limited, at best. The conundrum, of course, is that if you're not creating, why bother (to market or promote)?

A bit of a chicken–and–egg thing, that. But to my way of thinking, the art must come first. You can create without turning a profit (by choice or circumstance). Putting together the jigsaw puzzle of an illustration *career* and nimbly juggling the various pieces of the *job* depends on the clients that define your freelance *business*.

Job. Career. Business. If that's the goal, then it's off to market for you. And if you market, you must promote.

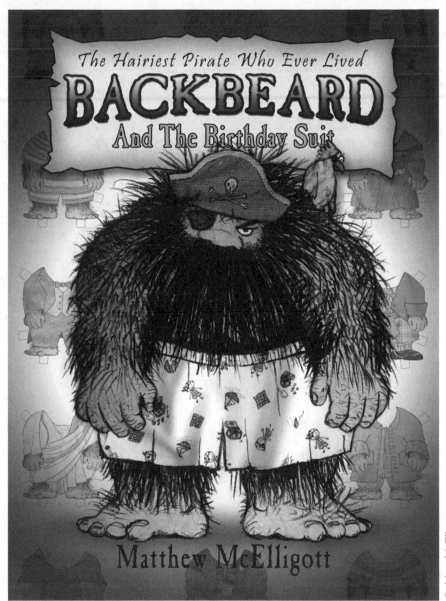

© Matt McElligott

9
Dealing with Failure

It takes a lot of experience to understand that when something is wrong, it's just another form of "right"—just not "right now."

—ILENE WINN-LEDERER,
  ILLUSTRATOR

The Best Teacher? "Failure," illustrator Lance King says, reiterating the universal sentiment of *every* illustrator I interviewed, "is really is one of the best teachers." The goal, of course, is to learn from your mistakes, to improve on the problem, and to influence future success.

In this chapter we will discuss what you can learn from mistakes and how you can benefit from failure. You will hear some common themes running throughout this chapter: that mistakes and failure are both inevitable but character building; that success is relative; and that coping skills (including preparation to meet the challenge of failure) are key components of your illustrator's skill set.

Let's see how we do just that.

© Ilene Winn–Lederer

Just Wrong

"We need to get away from machines and get back to the human and analog side of our world," David Julian believes. "Working digitally, errors in art making are virtually correctable," he says. " I don't have to scrape down paint or recut wood—I just undo in Photoshop's History or go back to a safe version."

And now the conversation takes an interesting turn. "But I don't believe there are any 'mistakes' at all," he comments. The reason being? "Many students come in fearful of making mistakes," he continues. "This gets in the way of problem-solving, which gets in the way of the pure joy of creativity. Mistakes are just exercises in our personal judgment."

Here, Julian goes on to question the very relationship of "wrong" and "right." "Why think you've done something 'wrong'? In reality, the mistakes you make invariably lead to better solutions. I regard 'mistakes' as process. The more work you do, the more you practice, the more these 'mistakes' integrate themselves into your normal process rather than into a deadline mentality."

Make It a Learning

"We get way more information out of mistakes than out of successes," Julia Minamata says. "What you learn from failure is completely dependent on what you're willing to take from the experience. The most important thing we learn from our successes is that success is possible.

"Any illustrator will tell you that one of the worst feelings in the world is when an art director kills a job," Minamata continues, "especially when you're just starting out! My very first official illustration gig was killed.

"Although I had already questioned my ability to build a career in illustration on many occasions, when I opened up the magazine and looked futilely for my piece, I wanted to crawl into bed and never leave.

"I still wrestle with self-doubt today, but I now understand that overcoming fears and insecurities and dealing with rejection are part and parcel of working in a creative field. There is a Zen saying that states, 'The obstacle is the path,' and I believe it."

"One of my clients," Ilene Winn-Lederer tells us, "was an international nonprofit organization that commissioned a book cover and interior chapter headers combining illustration and calligraphy.

"It was a dreaded case of 'art by committee.' The art director was wonderful to work with. However, she was bound to work with a tough, opinionated committee of nonartists who only knew what they didn't like (and whose input spelled the success or failure of my involvement with the project).

"In the months-long process, I turned out an historic (for me) thirty-nine revisions for the project, any of which the art director thought would be just fine. However, she was blocked by the committee, who nitpicked every detail, from color scheme to the position of or 'potential interpretation' of certain elements in the cover image.

The long, hard road of making your own mistakes to get to your final destination is always open to everyone at all times.
—ULANA ZAHAJKEWYCZ, ILLUSTRATOR

"Granted, they paid well—enough for the project—but ultimately, the end result was about as exciting as a neutered cat. The silver lining in this whole mess was the better contract that this client and I now work with. It sets a limit on revisions with a 'You want to play? You have to pay!' clause. And that means I charge my day rate per revision."

"Failure or disappointment is an education," says illustrator Mike Quon. "Even though you crave a challenge, you must live in the present. Go for the proverbial brass ring. Take the chances. But if the job is beyond your skill set, have the guts to move on to something else (big or small) if it doesn't work."

"And since this is called 'commercial art,' it has to get done," continues illustrator Stan Shaw. "Sometimes you succeed for your client but *fail yourself* as an artist. I always keep in mind that there will be another chance, another experiment. Prepare and broaden your skills (and outlook) for the next illustration. I liken it to wind sprints, training for a longer race."

Adult Swim

"Usually the first thing I do after reassuring the art director that I can handle this job—hey, no problem—is panic," says illustrator Tom Graham. A seasoned professional, Graham is reticent to admit it, but doesn't deny this fact—the anxiety of "being in deep water, up to my eyeballs" is *very* real.

After about an hour, Graham says he settles down. "I read the text and start thinking—rationally and objectively. I again realize that solving an illustration problem is an intellectual as well as an artistic job (maybe more intellectual than artistic)." And then the fun kicks in and his confidence returns.

And illustrator Scott Jarrard owns up too: "I totally fear failure," he says. "I want to succeed. I want to be the best I can be. Failure is not an option. I keep on moving. I deal with failure by working harder. By taking a deep breath. By taking a break, pondering, doing the dishes, going for a walk. I'll do something else—and then go back and rework whatever my problem is."

Add to this that some folks feel there is a certain safety in failure. There's no pressure if you're convinced that you'll just blow the game, regardless. Why take the risk—you *know* the outcome. So you don't take the shot (or you dog it), certain of the results. And sure enough, the self-fulfilling prophecy comes true.

Jarrard tells you to wholeheartedly learn from your mistakes. "Hopefully, by accepting a mistake, I can avoid making the same mistake again," he points out. "If I can now avoid that same mistake, I have progressed. If I have progressed, it means *I am learning*.

"If I am learning, then I am enjoying life. If my life were 'easy,' or if I didn't struggle professionally, I would be shortchanging the future. By recognizing my faults *and* my progress, I have something to look forward to—I look forward to being a better person and a better artist."

Damage Control

When you really blow it, how do you face that fact? In these instances, the recovery process becomes the immediate priority. Ya gotta *deal*. But not

© Michael Fleishman

asking for enough money, or being cheated by a client, is a completely different sort of error than misjudging a job, not satisfying the client, or doing poor work because you're overbooked.

To clarify and organize, let's break down our damage-control report into separate categories: money mistakes, artistic failings, and logistical or mechanical mistakes.

MONEY, MONEY, MONEY

"My business education was learned on the job," Dan Yaccarino recalls. "I made *a lot* of mistakes. Everybody gets cheated. Everybody loses money from some dumb decision that they make; I've certainly had my share of those.

"Early on in my career, I sent out a promotional postcard (which I didn't bother to copyright). Just by chance, a friend of mine who owned a bookstore happened to get a catalogue from a small publisher. Sure enough, there was my image on the cover of a book without my knowledge or permission.

"I called my lawyer, who recommended that I have a copyright lawyer draft a letter for me, which I sent to the publisher. I met with them and, after I threatened to sue, the publisher paid me for running the image in his catalogue (and the book was not released with my image on its cover)."

Yaccarino says he tried to learn from mistakes like this one. He advises you to note how and why certain enterprises don't take off, to be very conscious of exactly what happened.

"Yes," he admits, "this is standard advice for pretty much everything, but in this context, we're talking about our careers. So examine your motivation, look hard at both your failures and successes—sit down and take a good, long look.

"Over the years, a few of my images have appeared in package designs, and I really wanted to do more of that. I spent an enormous amount of time and energy mocking up several designs and laid out a lot of money to get them professionally shot. However, nothing came of it. I was very disappointed.

"This is not to say that I shouldn't have tried to get work outside the scope of my usual assignments. But I refused to accept that there was an actual reason I wasn't getting that type of job. In reality, either it was a trend toward other work, the result of the economy, or that my work wasn't terribly suited to package design."

"Early in my career," Winn-Lederer says, picking up the conversation, "I was commissioned to create a series of large drawings to grace the restaurant walls of a major hotel chain. Excited about this 'showcase' opportunity, I agreed to the conditions of the project without looking too closely at the details.

"The commission came through a local art consultant who led me to believe that the price quoted was to cover the cost of each drawing. After an intense couple of months, the drawings were completed and delivered.

"I came down with a nasty case of the flu and thereafter learned that the check I received (which was only for a portion of the project) was in fact the only money I would ever see.

"Furious, I called the art consultant, who smoothly reminded me that the hotel chain was *her* client and that they would pay no further on the project. So unless I wished to file a lawsuit (the consultant's husband was a big-time attorney), which I couldn't afford to do, I was simply madder and wiser for my experience.

"By the way, I later discovered other artists who had been badly treated by this 'consultant' and will no longer work for her. She now hangs cheap posters in obscure hospital corridors."

"I have definitely made my share of mistakes," Ken Meyer, Jr., tells us, continuing the thread, "working both freelance and full-time.

"At a day job for an online gaming company, I made two mistakes. While moving from one project to another, I was asked to do work for which I hadn't been hired (and was not trained properly).

"I should have done two things: (1) Applied myself more intensely, hopefully picking up what a fellow employee attempted to teach me (with the little time and enthusiasm he had available). (2) I should have argued louder for real training and the time to do it. The result? I lost that job, possibly the best job I ever had.

"As a freelancer, I recently worked on an assignment for cards based on a popular online game. The art director I was working with was passing comments on to me from his superiors but not editing them at all.

"As a result, I got incredibly rude and derogatory comments from these people and it affected my work. In fact, after completing (and redoing) several pieces, I was dropped from completing the remaining pieces.

"I should have pointed out more vehemently that these unfiltered comments were uncalled for. And I shouldn't have let such comments get to me in the first place.

"But you know," Meyer says, as he sums up this lesson, "if you always succeed, you are not really learning. In hindsight, I also realize that this was a job I should just have passed on."

With admirable candor, Meyer will admit, "I don't think I've completely recovered from losing that online gaming job. Hopefully, with time, I will get over it and learn from the experience even more. As for the freelance gig: I need to take a closer look at *every* job I accept and not just concentrate on the money (albeit much needed) the project will bring in."

MECHANICAL DIFFICULTIES

"I have learned to walk away from a problem when the answer is not revealing itself after an honest effort," says Lizzy Rockwell. "It is impossible to be creative and frustrated at the same time. Frustration can be agonizing, but I trust the solution will ultimately come to me.

"I was working on a series of five illustrations for a toy company creating covers for girls' writing journals," Rockwell tells us. "The creative director hired me because she thinks I am capable of creating 'soulful' characters. She wanted these covers to be an antidote to the shallow, overtly sexual, and overly aggressive images of girls (and women) that eight- to twelve-year-old girls are besieged by.

"The title of the journals reads, 'Thoughtful Girls.' Each girl is of a different ethnic background, and each has a different muse or hobby. They are shown at a table with the journal in front of them, pencil poised or writing, and looking . . . well, thoughtful!

"The first character I came up with was based on the creative director's nine-year-old daughter, who is just this type of wonderful girl; charming, with fun-to-draw braids down to her waist.

"I know her but had photos to work from and a memory of her expressions and personality. I am not realistic, but the real-life reference point was a nice place to start. Also, I usually draw kids a few years younger than this, so reference was helpful.

"The creative director loved the drawing. Great—but I now set a high bar to meet for the next four characters. It was hard, partly because each girl had to express the prerequisite qualities in a completely different way, and also because they had to come across as individuals with unique personalities, cultural backgrounds, and interests.

"Trying to capture something as wispy and fleeting as 'soulfulness' and 'thoughtfulness' is not as easy as you might hope! Showing someone alone and still (with all her action internal) is sometimes the hardest thing to draw. It comes from an intuitive place in the mind. No amount of good drawing, rendering, reference material, filling wastebaskets, or grinding down pencil lead will bring the solution.

"So this was one of those assignments that I had to walk away from once in a while to get back on track. But I loved the assignment so much. I loved these girls I was creating, I loved the expressive young ladies who would someday fill these journals with their thoughts. I never lost patience. And I am experienced enough to know that the solution will come if I let it."

Communications Skills and Customers

Good communication skills—right from the very start of the job—are vital. The illustrator should strive to talk over concerns before any drawing begins; this helps to prevent potential problems in the long term.

Jarrard says another consideration (and an important part of damage control) is to just consider how much time a fix or change will take. "If it isn't a ton of time, I will just get it done. The one or two hours it will take to make the change aren't worth losing the client."

Fickle customers—clients who completely change their minds after seeing the final—are presented a supplemental bill. "Have it all written out in a contract before the project even begins," Jarrard says. "This will usually help avoid problems during the job. I have learned from experience to work everything out in the agreement."

© Rick Sealock

ARE WE HAVING FUN YET?

Of course, once the job is signed, the real fun of working on commission begins. "I am a complete and total people pleaser," admits Jarrard, who quickly adds, "But that isn't a good business character trait to have.

"I'm in business for the long term and I need to develop long-term clients to be successful. That means trying to make my clients happy.

"When mistakes happen, my first reaction is flat-out anger. I'm a perfectionist and I *really* hate not getting things right the first time. But once I settle down a bit, I can honestly analyze the situation. I'll ask myself a lot of questions: 'Exactly what was my glitch? How did I blow it—where did I go wrong? What was the client expecting?'

"If it was truly my fault, and I was completely off track, I'll start over and suck up the time. If we're in a gray area, I will talk to my clients to hear their concerns, and *then* I'll share my point of view. I can talk the client through my process and concept to explain why I did certain things. Many times we'll come to a happy middle ground once each of us has shared his expectations."

This part of the job—and a big part of bouncing back peacefully—involves learning when to go forward and knowing when to pull back (or in another direction).

As PJ Loughran points out, "A big chunk of this self-knowledge is a sense of humility. This is the awareness of your strengths and your shortcomings—and never forgetting either," Loughran says. "It's the opposite of entitlement. No matter how talented you are, regardless of how easy it all came to you, just because you are good (or *great*) at something, doesn't mean people should (or will) be throwing money at you. Arrogance is a dangerous thing.

"Everybody makes mistakes. Especially in a creative discipline, you're never going to knock it out of the park every time. Everybody does both good and bad work, but the way to bounce back is to be consistent over the long haul.

"So if you make a mistake," Loughran sums up, "you pick yourself back up. This mistake shouldn't be the end of your career. The industry is quite forgiving, as long as the quality of your work is consistently good."

Branch out and go out on that limb, too. The old cliché may be shop-worn, but is still a truism. Mistakes are always an occupational reality, but so are lofty goals and great success.

"I enjoy testing my limits to see how far I can take things (personally, artistically)," Loughran tells us. "I enjoyed the challenge of becoming an illus-trator; it is not an easy thing to do. Same thing with pursuing my musical career. It was, 'I can do this—now *how far* can I run with this?'

Says Loughran: "I never want to say 'I could've' or 'I should've.' I want to be able to say 'I did' or 'I didn't.' There's something satisfying in that—even if it doesn't work."

10

When Bad Things Happen to Good Illustrators

You are invariably off balance, but you have the aim.

—PAUL MELIA, ILLUSTRATOR

Hey, That's Tough!   Most illustrators I know will tell you that, in many respects, this is one tough business. Why be an illustrator if it's such a hard slog? Feeling this way, in the face of adversity you might rightly ask: "What are the reasons I'm doing this?" Maybe you even ask it right out loud, and to no one in particular.

Me? I do it because I love (and have always loved) making art. I'm following my dream and passion; my art *career* is actually a sublime bonus.

But I also realize that I want to hang in there for the long haul. And I want to provide for my family doing just what I am doing. Not only that, but

SNiFFiNG CAN HARM YOUR Nervous System.

CONVULSIONS aside, IT's NOT THAT bAD.

USING INHALANTS TO GET high MAY NOT kill you, JUST A FEW NERVES. You KNOW, The ONES THAT control things LikE SPEECH ANd bREATHING. DEAD NERVES ARE LikE DEAD PEOPLE, THEY DON'T COME BACK. Visit www.drugfreeamerica.org FOR MORE INFORMATION.

PARTNERSHIP FOR A drug-FREE america©

© Paul Dallas

I want to grow and diversify; to stay open to all opportunities; to be an entre-preneur (even if I can't spell or pronounce it right).

The daily grind of the illustrator can take its toll. Certain physical, mental, and emotional aspects directly result from a (hopefully) long life at the drawing board. And then, of course, life is way out of our control. Accidents, tragedy. Fate, destiny. Good luck getting out of this alive!

It's inevitable—we all rust or flame out. And then stop. Whenever. Wherever. But until you come to that full stop, you want to make the most of everything you got going at the drawing board.

This chapter is about an illustrator's endurance. Endurance means action and determination, focus and dedication—all tempered by the ability to bounce softly when you're up against it.

Let's talk about being good to yourself, especially when bad things happen to good illustrators.

Rest Your Eyes, Refresh Your Mind, Relax Your Body

Illustrator Ali Douglass's creative vision is 100 percent, but she is having some physical issues with her eyes. Her condition affects the work, but it's not because of the work.

In her care and treatment, Douglass learned something many artists don't realize—her problem is exacerbated by not blinking all the way down. "I'm only blinking halfway. That is a learned behavior caused by staring at the computer too long or focusing on your illustration so intensely. Do this enough, and you train yourself to not blink completely; you blink halfway and come right back up. Your eyes become really dry by not blinking enough, and that can lead to other problems down the road.

"You have to take a break every twenty minutes and focus far out, thus protecting your eyesight. That is something I've had to learn and practice. Take five; stretch your body out, focus somewhere else other than that three-inch hot zone.

"Another thing—I use triple-zero brushes. When you hold a brush this fine, all of your arm is engaged. Do this all day long, most of the week, and after a while specific muscles are going to squawk. Other muscles kick in to compensate and relieve the strain, but in the process, they are overtaxed. It's a vicious cycle.

"I'm twenty-nine and I feel like I should be invincible, but of course, I'm not." And to the reader of these words, a friendly caution—you are not, either.

Digital Blues

On the road to writing this book, I swerved on a slippery patch of health mishaps. The events as they unfolded hit like buckshot, but I ultimately dodged much bigger bullets.

Around Thanksgiving, I lacerated my right thumb pretty badly with a kitchen knife. My Butterball moment was just a stupid thing on my part, but that's why they're called accidents. And here I was facing one of my all-time, bowel-clenching fears—I had just sliced up my drawing hand.

The initial loss of normal hand strength, control, and skills was a mind-blower. Even simple tasks were complications (and are still often painful reminders). I briefly became a hardship lefty out of pure necessity. Humility, thy name is Charmin.

Hairy as it seemed, it could have been far, *far* worse. I carved deep enough, but actually *missed* the major tendon and nerves by that same hair.

Despite all my kvetching and worrying (both real and imagined), I was actually a rather lucky (albeit clumsy) illustrator.

SHELL SHOCK

Then, maybe a month later, came an episode with a viral infection of the inner ear. There is a wee gizmo of your inner ear called the "labyrinth." It's shaped like a snail's shell and it's sort of like a gyroscope for your brain.

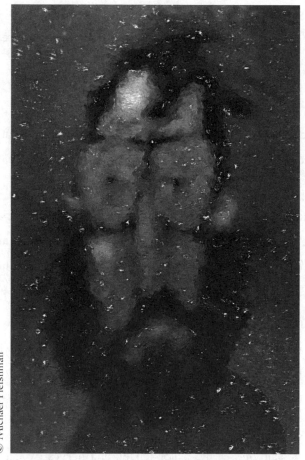

© Michael Fleishman

Labyrinthitis (what I really had) is an irritation and swelling of that structure. But all the symptoms it brought on—vertigo, loss of balance, cessation of movement, hearing loss, nausea—make it look like you are having a *stroke* (what we all *thought* was going on). And therein lies the tale of a scary ambulance ride, a night in the ER, and many tests I can only half remember.

I soon heard about a number of other guys in the Dayton area who had the same experience: same ailment and, thankfully, the same outcome. And then came the news of a relative who wasn't so fortunate: same symptoms—but an actual, major stroke.

THIS IS IT

Fast forward to Christmas of this year (at this writing), when I learned I had to have my appendix out. Sheesh . . . I thought I was too old for these things. Ha!

So what's my point here? Besides fully acknowledging my little blessings, I was reminded that control is ephemeral, that it only takes one moment for "all that" to change to "all this," and then you have to just deal.

I accepted help with gratitude. I tried to be more aware of what I could do and could *not* do (and worked to keep each action in its own state of grace). I acknowledged frustrations and owned my fears and attitudes. And—especially in the middle of my "run of bad luck"—I saw that it all could be really, truly, absolutely, much worse.

However, for some people, the superlative "worse" is relative. Let's talk to just two.

Bethany

Bethany Broadwell tells you she's one of the fortunate few. "I can honestly say it was a practical decision for me to become a freelance artist," she states.

She's thirty-something, weighs a mere forty pounds, and has a neuromuscular condition called spinal muscular atrophy. The disease progressively weakens Broadwell's physical strength and causes her to rely on a wheelchair for mobility. A simple task like speaking on a telephone or arriving to an appointment on time involves massive organization and planning. Completing every aspect of even the simplest effort usually means she must depend on someone to help.

Broadwell is not an illustrator; she's a Web designer who works with images on a daily basis. She battles massive physical challenges, but her eye for design is solid and her ideas strong (in fact, she did my wife's Web site, and helped me brainstorm my Web site as well).

"I create a representation in Web site elements (and words) that reflects the message or impression my clients want to convey. It is a formal way of saying that I help people express themselves by supplying them with the 'just right' finished project." So, like a good illustrator, she is in the business of solving communication problems.

"I need enough flexibility in my work routine to maintain my stamina," she says. "It made sense for me to seek out home-based employment that can largely be accomplished in front of a computer."

As her arm and hand movement is extremely limited, technology makes it feasible for Broadwell to circumvent these challenges. Her fingers never pass over a keyboard. "I strictly use the mouse and click key by key on a virtual, on-screen keyboard," she tells us.

"Once I am positioned in front of my system, I can work independently, for the most part. My favorite communication methods are e-mail or instant messages, because they offset my slightly unclear speech and allow me to interact with clients."

Working on a project basis gives Broadwell the leeway to attend to any personal-care needs she may have. "As long as I keep careful watch on my deadlines, I can complete assignments at my own pace. Providing I meet or exceed my clients' expectations, the matter of how or when I accomplish their project is immaterial."

Pushing practicality aside, however, Broadwell feels it is more interesting to reflect on why artistic freelance projects can be a good match for people with disabilities. "In my case, the main philosophical reasons have to do with the three C's of control, connectivity, and continuance.

"The reality is I can get a little down if I dwell on my physical condition being out of my control. When I am disheartened by my limitations, my art can help me cope with these helpless feelings. It gives me the power to shape images into the creative arrangement of my design. I have an outlet I can mastermind."

Broadwell admits that her work also pushes her to be more outgoing. "A disability can contribute to a sense of separateness and inadequacy," she says. "In order to keep my flow of projects steady, I am constantly networking, brainstorming, and asking questions to stockpile creative leads for future endeavors.

"I am put into a position of needing to take initiative, exude confidence, and demonstrate my capabilities. The repetition of these tasks helps me become a more vibrant, positive contributor.

Does she feel she has a calling, that she is "making a difference"? "This is the mission of all kinds of people," she ponders. "As someone deemed 'frail,' the idea of impacting others is a factor I contemplate. How can my small self influence others in a positive way, when my existence itself is so precarious? Through art, I am comforted to think that I am creating a means of continuance. Whether I am here or not, my perspective is established."

Erin

Do you want to talk about coping skills and bouncing back? Let's chat with Erin Brady Worsham, who points out that disability is a possibility for all of us. "If nothing else," she says, "it brings about the profound realization that art was never really about the pencil and paper or the paintbrush and canvas. Whatever the challenges, artists will find a way to express themselves." Not just Pollyanna talk and another smiley-face moment, folks. Worsham knows.

"I was an artist before I got sick, but my work lacked focus," she tells us. "When I was diagnosed with ALS [amyotrophic lateral sclerosis] in 1994, I knew it was only a matter of time before I would no longer be able to use my hands, and I lost the need to create. It was only after I found out I was pregnant that I wanted to live and make my mark on the world for my child.

"Thinking that visual expressions were beyond me, I began to paint images with words on my communication device by writing a journal for my son. I think this was an important period for me, because it forced me to fine-tune my descriptive skills.

"In 1999, when we discovered how I could work on the computer, my mind went wild with the possibilities. I had taken the simple act of putting

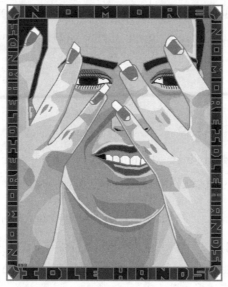

© Erin Brady Worsham

pencil to paper for granted. Now I have to use a painstaking process with a sensor taped between my eyebrows, but it seems a small price to pay to draw again.

"I am confused when people ask how I cope, because I don't see the alternative. I am as I am, and I am who I am, and that is an artist. My art has given me an identity outside of the ALS. It lifts me above the physical limitations in my life to a place where I can work—just like any other artist.

"There is also an irony here. Most people would see me working at my computer and think I am working alone. But in my mind, that's when I connect to the world. My disability makes spontaneous, face-to-face conversation almost impossible. And often, people find it difficult to look past the visual effects of my disease to realize I'm on a par with them mentally. "Because of this, I prefer to have my conversations via e-mail. On the computer I am just like anyone else. No one need ever know I even have a disability, and I can let my work speak for itself. For a time I was part of a computer art group out of Australia. The funding eventually ran out, but it was wonderfully stimulating while it lasted. We were given themes and assignments. Like in art school, it made me produce."

Wrestling with That Ego

What other "disabilities" do illustrators put in their own way? For instance: How do you deal with self-created demons?

In a recent interview, I was asked to cite my biggest professional failure (and how I overcame it). But for me, this isn't a specific event. From my point of view, it's the challenge to resist the tricks ego can play with your self-perception.

Talk about monsters under your bed! For better or worse, the quest for recognition, approval, and rewards (not to mention the bucks) is a part of an illustrator's reality. The competition is fierce in this field, the level of ability out there is simultaneously intimidating and inspiring. Accolades and achievements are certainly desirable, undeniably cool, insanely great, and guaranteed to clear your complexion while improving your SAT scores at the same time (maybe just *half* a joke). But that's not what being an illustrator is *really* about; that's not really why you draw and paint, is it?

Well (to me, at least), it *shouldn't* be—you do art because you *love* it. You create because of the little rush (and big tickle) you get when you realize, "I made this. *Me*. No one else can do it quite this way."

There will be inevitable moments when you need to remind yourself of that. And getting to that actual heart of the matter is what's REALLY desirable, cool, and insanely great. However, I'm still working on my complexion and improving my SAT scores.

Fight or Flight

Around the late nineties, life (professionally and personally) got more than a bit daunting. I had a stretch where business spiraled down. Nothing was happening; the illustration work was evaporating, and writing jobs dropped off. My teaching job simply sucked. It was somewhat of a dry spell on steroids, actually.

I could sit around to piss and moan, or I could do something about this mess. So, I worked hard to keep the faith, to actively make changes or upgrades on all fronts. And if you are reading these words, I am here to say that I turned it around.

How? I can sum it up in three words: *resolve, action,* and *diversification.* I had diversified early, and I am a firm believer that work begets work; that it is easier to find work when you have work. I could now pull my thumbs out of a number of pies: I was illustrating, teaching, and writing; there were small-scale school and library visitations, plus larger scale speaking gigs.

I'll risk sounding like a late-night TV commercial to say that a good attitude (and positive mindset), strong work ethic, and active marketing and promotion make the difference. It did for me (and I'm not going to say "at least," as it was hardly a minimal effort). I believe it can for you, too.

So could I be working the midnight shift at the local mattress warehouse? Sure. And while that is honorable work, I had different ambitions. And so did Ray-Mel Cornelius, an illustrator and teacher, who tells us, "A student once told me he was having a hard time deciding whether to enter the communication arts or go into business with his uncle, who had an air-conditioning/heating repair business.

"I told him that there was nothing wrong with A/C and heating repair, and if he felt he could make that choice, then A/C and heating might well be for him. I would have made a terrible A/C and heating repairman, and probably a terrible just about everything else. There's nothing else I could or would want to do with my time other than make images."

Distractions

What? I'm sorry—I got pulled away for a second. Now *where* were we? Ah, yes—how do you deal with distraction?

"I deal with distractions by hiding in my office," Scott Jarrard says, laughing. "I have a home office and I absolutely *love* being able to spend time with my wife and kids. But if I need to get a project done, I will turn on some tunes and shut my office door. If the door is closed, my family knows not to bother me.

"If my wife wants the family to go camping and a client calls with a rush job that can't wait, she knows that the clients are paying the bills, and we'll go camping tomorrow night. So I try to deal with my distractions by prioritizing my client's needs along with my family needs."

Looking at the big picture of *all* of your responsibilities is just plain smart, and establishing priorities is wise indeed. Think about it: A "distraction" can be considered as such only if your priorities aren't straight.

Tough Love

So, this is one tough business. But you're one tough illustrator, right? It's certain that adversity will rear its ugly little head over your long haul at the drawing board. And that's the operative phrase right there: the *long haul.* If time and luck are good to you, the long haul means you will have opportunities. To make good. To cope and endure. To grow and learn.

And if you are good to yourself, the action, determination, focus, and dedication we discussed in this chapter won't be just idle cheerleading—it will be what you go to when you're up against it.

11
Big Changes

That's the wonderful thing about illustration: there's a definite need for it; you fit in with society, you have an important role.

—WARD SCHUMAKER, ILLUSTRATOR

Is This Any Way to Make a Living?   "These are tough times for illustrators," says David Julian. "The current economy has made it tougher for companies to afford better illustration and pay the way they should be paying. Illustrators work harder for the same amount of money.

"The pool has gotten huge. Technology has enabled many people to compete on a level that would've been more difficult had it just been about talent alone. A lot of stuff is out there because it can be."

If you've made it to this chapter, you've read numerous professional testimonials of how illustration demands a special commitment—the classic

definition of a particular calling. You've also read that, these days, it's not the easiest way to make a living.

As PJ Loughran says, "Perhaps there's not as much financial reward as there once was (maybe twenty, thirty years ago), but the rewards do still exist if you're willing to work hard, persevere, and be calculated in your approach."

In this chapter, we will discuss Loughran's thesis above. We'll also examine changes that have been wrought by the digital age. We'll look at how the use of stock and clip art (royalty–free images) has greatly changed the business.

Roots and Transformations

Let's first discuss Loughran's point that there was indeed more financial reward for illustrators in decades past.

In a July 1999 article at the Illustrators' Partnership of America Web site (*www.illustratorspartnership.org*), Brad Holland addressed the issue of stagnant prices. In his commentary, Holland makes some strong arguments. I recommend you visit the IPA site and read the whole piece, but let me summarize one of his main points.

"Thirty years ago," Holland writes, "some magazines paid artists as much as $800 for a single-page illustration. Playboy paid $1,600 for a double-page spread. Even an artist in his larval stage, as I was then, could make $12,000 for a big-budget movie poster.

"Now, multiply those sums by five to account for inflation and ask yourself: Where are the $4,000 magazine pages, the $8,000 spreads, the $60,000 movie posters? By stagnating for thirty years, prices have declined to one-fifth what they were then."

"This is a big issue," illustrator and educator Tom Graham says. "There are those who debate that illustration is no longer a viable career path. The God's honest truth is that no one has hard facts. Perception or reality? If you really want to dig, you might start at the Bureau of Labor Statistics or the last census or something."

Graham shares a common experience with many illustrators and points to a combination of factors. "In the late eighties," he relates, "I made a ton of money. Then there was a big slowdown in our business just after what some label the 1988–89 recession." (Author's Note: The word "recession" is loaded with meaning that may not be factual. We're not trying to paint the definitive financial history of this time period, just keep the conversation going.)

"And, of course, in 2001," Graham continues, "just before 9/11 (and certainly after), the volume of work eroded. Prices stayed flat or declined."

But back to '89. After the '89 period, Graham started to get ad agencies asking him to *bid* on jobs. "This indicated to me that content or style would not be the determining factor," he points out, "but price would be. This *never* happened before.

"By '89 you also had the first wave of Photoshop stuff coming along, as well as the whole stock–art issue. Also, don't forget about the relentless and wholesale realignment in magazines, ad agencies, and publishing—mergers, acquisitions, buyouts, layoffs, etc. The bean counters started ruling the world and budgets were scrutinized to maximize or eliminate every dollar spent. Eight conglomerates dictate how our world looks, what we read, what we listen to, what we watch. Am I paranoid?

"The real nail in the coffin may have been stylistic," Graham offers, "something that's harder to put your finger on. Assignment illustration, particularly in the high–profile venues, just went out of style (unlike in the seventies, which now looks like some sort of mini golden age).

"I know that many illustrators do about six different things for income. Gallery shows, lecturing, teaching, visiting elementary schools, children's books, per–diem production work (QuarkXPress, InDesign), furniture-making, crafts, kitchen design, all kinds of other non–art work.

"Illustration as a career lives," Graham insists. "But its practitioners have to be persistent, clever, entrepreneurial, dedicated. And there is a generation of talents out there that could care less about doing the cover of *Time* magazine. All that talent is bubbling away on zines and rock–show posters and graphic novels, blogs and gallery shows in off neighborhoods, working in tattoo parlors and low–budget film productions.

"And it's all going to rise to the top, eventually. The look of our culture will change. Again.

"If you trained as an automobile illustrator in the mid–sixties, hoping to get in on those big Detroit ad budgets, you'd soon be out of luck," Graham goes on. "Within a period of a few years, all those beautiful painted car ads disappeared, replaced by photos. The same is true for fashion and product print advertising in the seventies.

"So, is hand-drawn feature-length animation headed for oblivion since the string of successful digitally animated films? What happened to all those typographers? And those talented engravers before the halftone process allowed publishers to reproduce art and photos?

"An optimist suggests that for every door that closes, one opens. Alternate career planning may now be part of our required toolbox.

"History has one instructive thing to tell us for sure: Change in the business is a constant. As we are undoubtedly in the middle of changes now, it's helpful to realize that. The question to ask is: Are these changes permanent, or temporary? Unfortunately, the answer is: Who knows? We don't have the necessary historical distance to see.

"Clearly, this suggests other interesting dilemmas. For example, some illustrators feel stock illustration is killing the business, while other very knowledgeable pros suggest it's a harmless passing phase.

"Will editorial illustration return to substantial fees and contracts that are fair to both parties? Will mainstream periodicals tire of photography? Will the large multinationals win out, dictating fees and contracts on a take-it-or-leave-it basis?

"Will an educated, enlightened readership come back to the challenge of conceptual illustration? Can clothing retailers and manufacturers revisit the timeless romance and beauty of fashion illustration?

"In the 'golden age' of illustration, painterly realism with traditional drawing skills predominated. Such a style seems quaint today. Conventional talents may even seem a handicap in a world that values the outsider, the individual—the unique and crazy approach to looking at things.

"In a way, illustration was easier then; you knew what you had to learn, and there were benchmarks. Historically, much of what has been on the stylistic fringe has eventually been absorbed into the mainstream. So will traditional drawing skills be valued again? Maybe. But it won't be quite the same—it will be different, modern.

"If the 'cutting edge' is what's happening now, how much will be absorbed into tomorrow's mainstream?" Graham continues. "What is in style today will be out of style soon. So to chase the market is dangerous. The best advice is to follow your own interests and obsessions; be true to yourself. Do it well. Add to the mix. What comes out of that will then be unique.

"Strictly speaking, no knowledge of the history of illustration is necessary to be an illustrator. A smart approach, good conceptual skills, and a great eye and hand will carry the day. But I know of no successful illustrator who does not possess a knowledge of the basic history of American illustration.

© Tom Graham

"There are not many books that take a critical look at the history of illustration in America, but a good place to start is *The Illustrator in America: 1860–2000*, by Walt Reed, which surveys the major figures decade by decade."

Tighter Times

With over eighteen years in the business, Dan Yaccarino certainly has seen the business morph dramatically. "After 9/11, business got a little leaner," he says. "What once was a rather self-sustaining profession (in that a high percentage of artists were able to make a decent living without supplementing their income with anything else) really changed. Now, I hear from folks who were strictly editorial illustrators that this can no longer be done. This certainly reflects my personal experience as well.

"This stems from the economy, of course, but the whole general perspective is quite different these days. The audience is not terribly interested in an artist's interpretation of something. Viewers are looking for some sort of concrete imagery: no embellishment, no editorial perspective. Photography is being used more than ever. We're in a conservative time—conceptually, financially."

"It *is* different now," Isabelle Dervaux adds. "We should also mention that being an illustrator means a variable income. It's hard to plan ahead; there are elements you have no control over—health insurance, for instance, school tuition, the cost of housing. It's tough to make a living doing this (and to continue to do so)."

Part of the issue here is that the industry is certainly different, but part of it is that Dervaux is older. While it's true that the industry has changed, Dervaux and her needs have changed as well. That's a difficult thing to think about when you're young and hopeful, but it's something all artists, no matter what era they are born into, have to face.

And Dervaux agrees. "When you're young and single, maybe you don't need much. That's fine. But if you want to start a family, you find out that this is seriously *difficult*. Some illustrators can't make it without a spouse's 'regular' job (and benefits). That's staggering."

Here, PJ Loughran adds, "So there will be plenty of people out there telling you how risky it is and how 'most people' don't succeed.

"There's no quantifiable way to get there (like being a doctor or a lawyer). And as said before, most of us won't get very wealthy. It's not the right career if you want to be a rich man or woman," Loughran admits. "But it's still a viable career, and there are many people doing it—making a good living and living well."

Stock Questions

Stock art, it seems, is here to stay. At least, that's how I hear it in my informal and obviously limited poll of the illustrators appearing in this book.

We are throwing the word "stock" around, so let's clarify. "Stock," as defined by Holland at the IPA site, "is just a common name for the secondary rights to pictures.

"Selling stock requires an inventory of pictures," he continues, so "stock favors established artists, not beginners."

There are numerous stock-art houses selling stock illustration, and many illustrators choose to offer their own stock art to customers. Yes, the concept of stock (and secondary sales), whether sold by the individual illustrator or a business entity, is potentially lucrative.

But stock illustration competes with "assignment" illustration. Back at the IPA, Cynthia Turner defines assignment illustration as "an original

assignment [done for] a commissioning party [who] receives the rights to reproduce an illustration in a defined and limited manner."

So in a sense, illustrators selling their own back catalog compete against themselves, not to mention the stock images provided by a stock house (often sold for cheaper, and/or in bulk).

If you are selling stock, I'd rather you sell your stock as your private enterprise. For, as Holland describes, "A stock house is in business to make money for themselves, not for you . . . and if you conclude that it's a sound business decision to give inventory to a competitor that they can use to underprice you, then proceed accordingly."

"Royalty-free" is just that. To paraphrase tech jargon, it's a "buy once/use always" paradigm. Royalty-free art usually means a collection of images a buyer purchases and can exploit whenever, wherever, and however. All without your credit, with no regard to ethical considerations or production standards, and without further compensation.

Plus, the company that bought your illustrations (and released said collection) is actually (and legally) considered the creator of the work—you've forfeited all further rights to the art.

What's wrong with *that* picture?

STOCK ANSWERS

"My work has never been affected by my stock illustration," illustrator Lauren Redniss says. "I guess that is because I don't really do much actual illustration. My drawings are usually accompanying my own text, all integrated into one piece, so there is no room for any 'stock.'

"I work as much as possible by hand, which makes the process feel like creating art instead of completing a job. I find myself increasingly removed

from the world of illustration. The more I write and draw, the less marketable I become. There is very little place in the worlds of advertising, fashion, or even many magazines, based on my editorial stuff.

"I don't regret this because I have, instead, increasing opportunities to pursue my own work in books. However, I believe I could find a new balance that would allow me to balance the income and satisfaction of shorter-term projects with the more long and involved personal work."

"Stock fills a box that somebody wants to fill, and stock accommodates deadlines," Mark Braught says. "But because the answer already exists, I don't know how imaginative or inventive that solution is."

"And I don't think stock art is *the* great evil," Ward Schumaker chimes in. "I do know it *did* take a huge amount of work from us. But there were other things happening as well, and anyway, you can't stop it."

Dan Yaccarino agrees. "People point the finger at stock as the culprit, but I think that the industry will always evolve. It is never going to stay the same. Economics and technology affect any industry," he continues. "I'm sure there were a bunch of guys about a hundred years ago at the Society of Illustrators twirling their handlebar moustaches, upset about some new printing process. Those guys are all dead. The industry moved on and continues to morph. Folks complained about fax machines, and FedEx (e–mail, too). There were challenges then and there are challenges now."

Without making any judgment calls, Yaccarino is saying that—for better or worse—change is inevitable. Schumaker, Yaccarino, and Redniss are not advocating that you simply embrace stock art. Rather, they *are* saying to have an action plan. "It has to happen," Yaccarino points out. "You adapt or you become extinct. Swim or die."

LEMONS OR LEMONADE

"The market has changed," John Dykes says. "Some folks feel that this is a zero–sum game—that there is a set and finite number of assign–ments. The thinking goes: For each and every stock use, there is one less 'assigned' illustration.

"While stock use has definitely lessened the number of illustration assignments, it is not so cut–and–dried. Rather, the market evolves—it shrinks in some areas, while growing in others. I disdain the royalty–free market. But if there is anything positive about it, it has made it possible for certain segments of the market to open up and be receptive to using illustration in general. Some of these businesses eventually step up and need high-quality stuff, and they then assign something."

Dykes is a realist, however. "Yes, stock use has changed the world of assignment work, " he tells us. "It's more of a technological and global market change, and not some evil conspiracy taken on by the 'stock empire' that has caused this.

"In every aspect of commerce, people find faster and cheaper ways to produce. Artists are very sensitive to this dynamic. After all, it is their personal expression at stake. I wish there were ever-increasing room in this field for personal expression (i.e., great assignment work)—but there is less. Mix in the ever growing number of illustrators out there (and more 'committee'-determined choices for stock imagery), and clearly, it is a different place. Illustrators whose styles do not lend themselves to any secondary-rights usage are particularly uneasy, as they should be.

"It's a no-brainer that that's what's happened in photography. But, truth be told, stock has actually opened up markets for me. I'd much rather be doing only assignment jobs, but this is what's happening in the field. I can earn income from past illustrations, helping to ease those periods of slower assignment work."

OUT, DAMNED SPOT!

For other illustrators, stock is a definite call to arms. "At first, few of us saw the dangers of the stock-art dragon until it lifted its ugly head and started to devour the marketplace," cautions Rick Sealock. "Even I gave it a chance when it first started," he candidly admits, "till I saw its ugly side.

"The dream of stock art was that it served the industry, supplying ready-made illustrations for art directors with supertight deadlines. This would create more markets for the illustrator and promote higher illustration budgets.

"But soon the lower budgets started to happen," Sealock continues. "What actually went down was the selling of illustration work for *less* than commissioned work. Showcasing technically and conceptually weak illustration work came next, basically dumbing down the illustration field. If clients could get something cheaper and faster, who cared what it looked like or really communicated?

"How can that attitude help our industry? I say, Stomp it out! Send it straight back to hell! I even tried selling my own stock. I quickly discovered that even though it may be a cash cow, it was very unsatisfying.

"I love doing commissioned work, creating fresh images, facing new challenges, and learning more about our world in the process. Every new illustration gig means new ideas to communicate, new visual problems to solve, and having a blast!"

MOVING AT A FAST CLIP

"In the beginning, selling stock *was* kind of flattering and somewhat lucrative," Benton Mahan adds to the conversation. "There are a lot of good people doing stock but a lot of illustrators who feel that stock has hurt their business. Many magazines can't afford to buy illustration as they once did. Pay hasn't gone up any. The dividends from stock just kept going down."

And, as Dervaux points out: "Maybe a buyer doesn't have much money, so he wants stock. He looks at what's available and buys a number of different pieces (perhaps from different artists). So, (1) he puts your illustration next to images that may or may not work together, and (2) he's using old stuff—which means that (3) your work has changed. So the styles don't match, and the whole series is not unified.

"Or he wants stock but wants you to alter the image. The art director wants *this*, with a little bit of *that*. You end up with something that's mediocre at best. Plus, I don't want to redo what's already done—a job that's halfway between stock and original. You want the excitement of thinking out a new concept, not just repeating yourself.

"Some buyers are new to art direction or have a tough time art directing, so they buy something already 'in the can.' Assigning new art can be an issue when a client needs imagery for a presentation. New art is intangible, and the art director doesn't really know what he'll be getting in the end, so he goes an easier route."

Which, as the old saying goes, looks good on paper, but . . .

What a State We're In!

As mentioned in chapter 3, Benton Mahan sees the marketplace moving away from traditional illustration venues. "Previously, I did a lot of advertising and editorial illustration," he tells us, "but it's all changing. I can only speak for me, but I suspect that's just the way it is in general."

"Illustrators have to find a different way of doing business from even the nineties," James Yang says. "I remember before the Internet that sending your

portfolio to three different places a week was a very good week. Now my site gets hundreds of unique hits a *day*."

Like Mahan, Yang confirms that editorial illustration has seen better days. Magazines and newspapers—the traditional bread and butter of most illustrators—are in deep trouble because major advertising dollars are shifting from print to online media.

"The Internet, and the globalization of the marketplace, has caused intense pricing pressure. Many illustrators and reps mainly blame stock art for this, but I think they are missing the big picture," Yang tells us.

"The world is becoming more integrated, and with that comes the growing pains of this huge adjustment. Illustrators who understand how these changes affect them will adjust and do well. Those illustrators who can't adjust will have serious problems."

Yang feels that imagery must be considered a commodity these days. "Businesses will not pay much for generic images, but they will still pay for unique creative insight," he points out. "And this is not readily available."

Imagery must be accessible, or contact information must easily be found, on the Internet. An exceptional vision and an effortless, efficient delivery of that message make the difference. "Provide this, and you'll survive," Yang says.

"Selling more may just mean selling different," David Julian feels. "But one can also make the case for the classical business model: Be much more calculating in the subjects you choose to illustrate; target a style to specific buyers. Identify your audience, your client, and your market, and target your work to that. If you are talented and work the formula, you will be pretty successful."

ROLL AND BOUNCE

I think that to make better business your reality, you have to use the words "hope," "optimism," and "action plan" in the same breath. Embracing the phrase "change is good" as part of your working vocabulary is also smart (maybe "wise" is the more operative word).

"I think the current illustration field is regaining momentum," Douglas Klauba chimes in. "I've noticed the phone ringing more often. It's turning around again. I get this sense from talking to my rep and from the calls that are coming in. You can also see this by looking at magazines, at ads and brochures, and at the book market (but yes, it's true, there are only so many titles published in a year)."

While Mahan gets occasional calls for editorial jobs, he's currently doing children's illustration almost exclusively—and doing okay. Sam Viviano, art director at *Mad Magazine* (and formerly a prolific freelance illustrator), says, "I think the death watch for magazines is somewhat premature, but it's not premature to accept the fact that the magazine industry is changing vastly. Advertising dollars are shifting to broadcast media and the Internet. The rise of the focused, niche magazines means illustrators have to be conscious of market segments—but smart illustrators also will realize that there are *new* markets to tap into.

"It's important to start exploring other media," Viviano advises. "You must think of the Internet as a different medium than print. On a side note, maybe the biggest change for illustrators is the matter of technical distribution—and promotion—of the art (as opposed to the art itself).

"These days, art is being marketed, delivered, distributed, and viewed digitally. Truth is, I haven't met many of the artists working for *Mad* face-to-face. And I've never even seen their art on a *handheld* basis—it's sent to us via e-mail or uploaded to FTP sites. How they do the piece is irrelevant. I still don't see it in any kind of concrete fashion, I see images on a screen."

"My 'Op-Arts' are all drawings done on-site, then photocopied and collaged together with Scotch tape and Wite-Out," Redniss tells us. "Only at the last step do I use a scanner to import the piece, clean it up a bit in Photoshop, and e-mail it off.

"The photocopier is the fastest, simplest printmaking tool going. It gives a great, rich black (as long as the toner is fresh). It adds nuance and personality to a line, as opposed to a computer, which tends to sterilize things.

"I do, however, love how setting up a photo collage on the computer can save me so much time. I can mock together a number of elements in a flash, print them out, and work back into the image with drawings, photocopies, and other collaged elements. It is so easy to try a bunch of different ideas quickly on the screen and then work by hand only on the most promising concept."

Through Thick and Thin

We have been discussing the difficulties of being an illustrator in the modern world (largely because of computer, style, and delivery changes).

The various professional testimonials in this chapter examined the special commitment one makes to be an *illustrator*—even when that commitment doesn't translate into the easiest way to make a living. That commitment, however, does fit the classical definition for a chosen calling.

For a look at business practices and how illustrators are dealing with changes there, read chapter 5.

Shake It Up, Shake It Out

"The lines are blurred as to what an 'illustrator' can do," comments Mark Braught, "and I think the whole industry swings in and out, hot and cold." What do you do to stay in during those periods when it is a little colder than others?

"First, I think you look for different markets," Braught says. "Skills are the same—superior concepts and expert technique are still the benchmarks. But illustrators must be more entrepreneurial.

"The word 'blurred' in my statement stems from the introduction of the computer," continues Braught, "and the myriad of programs and filters these apps offer to the illustrator. For example, typography was formerly something many illustrators avoided in their compositions due to the sophisticated craft it represented. Illustrators can now create their own solutions (even dimensional type, such as wrapping text around objects or in perspective).

These days, you can dodge the high level of drawing ability needed to create such a solution. (Hey, even Norman Rockwell hired sign painters on occasion to do the typography for his sketches.)

The "blur" Braught brings up also refers to the generic job description of an illustrator. I'll speak generally: Advertising illustrators will try doing comic books. Editorial illustrators are working in children's books. Cartoonists tackle assignment illustration for magazines or produce graphic novels. Animation is huge: Assignment illustrators are creating shorts, and comic-book artists serve as production artists for major films. Fine arts (gallery shows and dealerships) is an interesting alternative. Teaching is an attractive opportunity. Licensing (using existing images to create cards, wallpapers, mugs, wrapping papers, notepads, etc.) is lucrative.

"We need to get comfortable with the fact that we make images," Braught states, "but one may wonder if there still is an establishment or such a thing as 'mainstream' illustration these days. We can see stuff people are doing all over the world now—and very quickly. That's fun. You get to see the whole *global gamut* of new talent coming up."

12
Communities

I have a really big neighborhood.
Whenever someone I know moves away
to a new town, I always figure the
neighborhood just got bigger.

—LORI OSIECKI, ILLUSTRATOR

Your Professional Community   In a previous chapter, Chris Spollen made the statement, "Your passion is what will define you." I'm repeating it because it is just so *true*. And once again, that gusto for your art (and hopefully, the lust for life) should be a no-brainer. But, as we also discussed in chapter 6, why go it alone? Passion can be absolutely infectious. And if social skills are your challenge, *then meet the challenge.*

"Create a *community* around you," PJ Loughran advises. "Get out—socialize. This can be an extremely isolating lifestyle. Even though that same isolation offers some considerable professional benefits, self-reliance becomes a bit dangerous if you get too good at it."

THE NEIGHBORHOOD

"At least half the people I socialize with are in this business," Dan Yaccarino says. "I know a lot of illustrators and writers, directors and producers, storyboard artists and designers, people like that. I'm definitely part of a larger artistic community."

And you could say that, in the illustration industry, networking is how *most* people get *all* of their work. It's who you know, folks branching out and reaching out. Referrals and repeat customers, promos that follow art directors jumping from job to job. "I've 'traveled' with many art directors," Yaccarino relates. "If they like working with you, you'll go with them from magazines to design firms to ad agencies to some Web thing. You'll go everywhere with them, if you have that good relationship."

Big-Time Karma

When I kicked off my illustration career, I networked at *every* opportunity. The Internet and e-mail were science fiction when I started out, so I did the legwork: I wrote letters, made phone calls, and paid visits when possible. I went to conferences and art shows, joined local art organizations, and became a member of the Graphic Artists Guild (on the national level).

My networking was very "traditional." Only, at that time, it wasn't considered "traditional," just "business as usual." While my methods would still work today (the intent and content of such communication is exactly the same), e-mail, blogs, and Web sites have changed contact and response time dramatically.

By and large, my letters made it to their destinations, but there was considerable lag time between contact and reply. I should also say that I preferred writing to cold calls on the phone. At that point of response, contacts could request to continue the conversation over the phone, or just stay pen pals (and I pursued either avenue earnestly).

If asked to cease and desist, I said, "Thanks for your time," and moved on. You never bat .1000, and these were busy professionals. Life is the ultimate final exam, and not all folks test well.

There is an ongoing correlation and connection between everything in the world that has existed, does exist, and will exist. You are part of that fabric of life.
—PAUL MELIA, ILLUSTRATOR

I was very interested in humorous illustration, as well as doing children's books, so I researched illustrators at the library and bookstores.

I phoned and visited local illustrators in my tristate area (Ohio, Indiana, and Pennsylvania). I tried to write to distant contacts directly, but if I didn't have a home address, I wrote to their publisher and asked them to forward the letter.

These letters were certainly fan letters in one sense—I did admire their work—but I took the opportunity to ask any and every question I could. I made it clear that I wasn't trying to steal the recipe to the secret sauce. Sure, we inevitably talked some shop—tools, techniques, toys—but I was mainly interested in the business end of the game.

And I learned a *ton*. Just about every illustrator I approached was extremely compassionate and gracious to a very new kid on the block. People gave me incredible advice and shared an amazing wealth of knowledge. They took time to discuss and review actual agreements (in some cases mailing me real paperwork, so we could do a point-by-point exploration of contract writing).

Yaccarino shares a similar experience. "People in this industry are very, very, very generous with their time and advice," he emphasizes. "I don't know of another industry that is so open and willing to help those getting into the business.

"Starting out, I would consult the annuals and call illustrators. If they were local, I'd go over and show my portfolio. I made a lot of connections that, twenty years later, *still* endure.

"Kids coming out of school, or making the rounds in the city, will call and ask if they can stop by. I am more than happy to spend some time and look at their work, to counsel or just listen."

Yaccarino believes in paying it forward. "I was there myself—and not that long ago. People were incredibly kind to me early on. I want to return that. I think it's important that we all do that.

"We're all together in this thing, and we all have to support each other," he comments. "I've never encountered an illustrator who has withheld advice when asked, and I've never turned anyone down, either."

Informal Formalities

If you're still at school (or just out), I'm going to suggest a nice baby step before you start looking for actual assignments or full-time work: the informal meeting.

Even if it's just a casual chat, I think there's a certain etiquette to follow when you get another illustrator (or an art director) to look at your work.

As far as art directors go, it's definitely harder to get a face-to-face meeting (or portfolio review) these days. People are just so busy (and it's much easier and more efficient to look at an online portfolio). Knowing that, if a one-time meet is the goal, I would be persistent: polite, gracious, accommodating, understanding—but stay at it.

Please note: I didn't say be a pain in the butt—don't write every week or e-mail (or call) every day. Make an initial inquiry and request to meet informally. Make it clear you're not looking to score a job or an assignment (or snatch hard-earned technical secrets on the cheap). Tell it like it is: You are just looking for feedback from a seasoned source.

If you are e-mailing or writing, and don't hear back in a week or two, write (or e-mail) again. Politely ask if the first message was received and repeat your request. If there's no response after the second request, reconsider the contact. *You* must decide how important this person is to your growth.

State upfront that you only want fifteen minutes (or whatever) on a specific date. Be right on time, and once you're in the door, *only take fifteen minutes* of the contact's time. Linger only if you are asked to stay longer. At the review, be a sponge. Listen more than you talk. Let your work do most of the talking for you. Keep the conversation professional.

Dress nicely. You could wear business attire, but in an informal meeting, what they call "business casual" is okay. Look serious enough about your good work to back it up with solid personal hygiene, too.

Show your gratitude and thank your contact for his time and trouble. Follow up with an e-mail (or better yet, a hand-drawn note) of appreciation. If warranted, ask to get together in some months to discuss (or show off) the fruits of the sage advice you just received. If you get a positive response here, follow up with a reminder closer to "show time."

If You Succeed, I Succeed

There are a lot of illustrators out there. It does seem like somebody let the word out that this is one of those proverbial "good jobs." Whoa! At times, it feels like it's "Everybody in the pool!" So, is diving into that pool like swimming with sharks and piranhas?

"I don't see a heavy-duty competition," Yaccarino insists. "Is it because, fundamentally, everybody's work is different? Oh, it's natural to feel envious at times, but I don't think there's any ill feeling at all. You just want everyone to succeed because it means there's *more* work for *all* of us. It'll revitalize the industry. It will bring back the notion of using illustration in advertising, TV commercials, and so on."

Will you find individuals whose views are not so humanitarian? Sure, but dawg, it doesn't *have* to be dog-eat-dog. Chris Spollen is one who feels exactly the same. "I *love* keeping in touch with fellow artists, " he says. "And if work comes my way and I feel it's more up someone else's alley than mine, I will pass it on. I'm always looking out for my friends, and I believe they do the same for me."

Take Heed

Savvy illustrators also know to seek input from sources outside the creative neighborhood. Advice and critique from other artists, family, and friends (even fans, when appropriate) can be invaluable. Ultimately, your art director (or editor) isn't the only one who will look at the work. "It's a good idea to determine whether the general public will understand your work as well," says Spollen.

Why is it good to seek the opinions of others? It's somewhat of a conundrum. While you know (or should know) your process and product best, you can get so invested in your art that you lose a certain perspective.

"I can't 'see' my work that well," Paul Melia says candidly. "But my wife can. When I work on a job, I'm too close to it to see it *objectively*. She hates to criticize me, though. She feels she's hurting me. But she's actually doing me a favor by telling me what's wrong with something so I can correct it. That's a helpful process."

That objectivity Melia mentions is the key, as I would seek contributions from any number of outside sources. Family and friends can make great focus groups, if they will give you an honest critique (and not just pat you on the back).

Obviously, I'd ask colleagues to evaluate your stuff. Not just fellow illustrators; I'd also go to artists outside your arena for a fresh angle. I'd approach folks removed from your peer group, too—both younger and older, professional and layperson.

Students will jump at the opportunity to "turn the tables" on you. This ready bunch can offer a fair review. But do find students without an agenda or an axe to grind, who are brave enough to be objective without kissing up or looking for "payback."

How should the illustrator listen to such feedback? That's an easy one: in the same manner you expect your evaluators to respond to the work, which is honestly, objectively, and without baggage. Remember, critiques are truly an invaluable resource, and you're not exempt from your good advice. A critique is not personal; it's an art review. It's all about how to improve the image. Your process and product are not so precious that you can't learn from (and survive) a direct, reasonable evaluation.

Stay in Touch

As I indicated in a previous chapter, even if they do their best stuff in isolation, illustrators need contact—professional, as well as personal, contact.

Most illustrators (including designer–illustrators) I know don't *choose* to be alone. You may lead (or be part of) a full–time staff. If you pursued a freelance career, it's most likely because you decided to work for yourself, but that doesn't—or shouldn't—make you a hermit. In any scenario, laboring alone is an occupational hazard we work with (or work around).

My friends are a great source of creative energy for me. A lot of them appear in my art. Consciously or unconsciously, people I know just show up in spirit or in actual images.

—LORI OSIECKI, ILLUSTRATOR

"At this point in my life, all the friends I have are like me, involved in many creative projects and building careers," Susanna Pitzer states. "Thank goodness for e–mail, so we can keep in touch.

"Since we are all reluctant to leave our work spaces to socialize without purpose, we have found that the best way to keep in face–to–face contact is to do projects together or to meet to critique work. I realize this sounds pathetic," Pitzer says, "but it's working for us."

"Like Susanna, I'm also not sure that illustrators, as a group, are loners," Tuko Fujisaki contemplates. "I have always sought the camaraderie of fellow professionals. It's just nice to be around people who understand what you do.

"And like Pitzer, when I lived in San Diego I was in a group of illus–trators that would meet at least once a month. More importantly, we would probably talk by phone almost daily. We called ourselves 'Joined at the Hip.'

"We would come up with group promos. By advertising together, we thought we could defer costs, but it was really a fantastic excuse for us to get together for the camaraderie.

"We spurred each other on creatively. I think it was just a wonderful time for all of us because we were all at a similar point in our careers. Two of us eventually relocated (and unfortunately, one member has passed away), but we have stayed in touch and are still good friends—and great fans of each other's work."

Coincidentally, Ken Meyer also had a somewhat similar situation when he lived in San Diego (maybe it's something in the ocean air). "I had a shared studio space with five or six other artists, mostly comic-book guys," he says.

"Although I was doing comparatively less work than they were, it was a great situation in which to get comments and feedback, see other methodology, etc."

Chris Spollen agrees. "Try to maintain a group of art-related friends who share your passion," he advises. "Make it a point to get together once a month for a dinner to talk shop. You must work to be social. You will start to eat the dates off the calendar if you do not make some form of human contact."

I've worked on staff and I've worked alone. Throughout the years I've juggled this combination in varying ratios, but all my jobs—teacher, writer, artist—stem from a commitment to my illustration career.

Teaching, writing about, and practicing the craft of illustration means I am a busy guy. I am daily and deeply immersed in the creative life. Very much like you, I'd bet.

I've had to make sure I get out there and maintain relationships and contacts (both professionally and personally). It is too easy to get wrapped up in the job. It takes some energy to get out of the studio, but it's a crucial aspect of the gig—and like I said, I'm committed to the gig.

Howdy, Pardner

So, how to "join the club" personally and professionally? What makes a colleague? How does one become (and stay) a colleague—are there rules and guidelines? Can one step over (or blur) the lines of personal or professional relationships? Are there rules of collegiality or boundaries of professionalism? Good questions, compadre, and the answers to these questions are easy.

Colleagues may be folks in your age group or contemporaries of any age group. They might be classmates, or part of a social group—folks you met at the gym or over coffee somewhere. You may kibitz with them at the water cooler during work hours.

These are peers with whom you share a common personal and/or professional bond. You focus on the same goals as equals. (Don't get hung up on talent or skill levels when evaluating a colleague, as this defeats the purpose of establishing that relationship.) On the job, a colleague can become a collaborator.

I don't think there are formal rules to maintaining collegiality (you probably figured it out back in your sandbox days as a kid). Staying a colleague means working to maintain that shared bond, to feed the professional association for the common good.

And like any affiliation, you can smudge or go beyond the boundaries of the relationship, but striving to be fair, honest, objective, and friendly should go far to avoid any pitfalls.

And by that same token, how many "best friends" can one possibly have? Is one enough? Are fifty not enough? Is it better to have twenty casual acquaintances or one good friend?

"A few best friends is great for me," Fujisaki says. "But not too many. It can be too distracting. Even when illustrators don't have work, we still always have things to do or should be doing (like updating your Web site, and getting promos out—two things I should be doing right now)!"

Here, Fujisaki takes a moment to reflect on family and friends. Is it important that her family and friends understand who she is and what she does? "I think my family 'gets me,'" says Fujisaki. "My mom thinks I'm pretty lucky that I have directed my life instead of someone else directing it. But it's not so important to me whether they get me or not, as long as I get me and am happy with me."

"My family is very proud of what I do," Pitzer chimes in, "and I involve them in many of my projects. I have some great nieces and nephews, and many of my stories and characters are based on them. They are my inspiration, my reviewers, my first audience . . . and in some cases my collaborators."

"Despite the early years, when I had to work really hard to train them," Ilene Winn–Lederer says, "I can say that my family makes an honest effort to

© Tuko Fujisaki

understand my work. Yet"—she stops to consider—"even when they affect an attitude of tolerance, the impatient vibes are loud and clear.

"Or is that my own guilty conscience whining? Ah, art is such a cruel master. . . ."

Joining the Club

Although I highly recommend joining art organizations and I strongly endorse the Graphic Artists Guild, I understand that wearing gang colors (metaphorically) is not for everyone.

But do consider your local illustration society (or design club). And definitely look into national organizations like the Guild (*www.gag.org*), Illustrators' Partnership of America (*www.illustratorspartnership.org*), Society of Illustrators (*www.societyillustrators.org*), AIGA (*www.aiga.com*), ICON (*www.theillustrationconference.org*), etc. These associations all have a common charge—the preservation and advancement of the profession for the good of the membership. The fellowship is invaluable, too—don't discount that.

These days, through the global forums of the Internet, you can network electronically. No jacket required: 24/7 access means prime opportunities for you—all without getting out of your pajamas, if you prefer (but remember, you must sleep *sometime*, and it's still crucial to get out of the studio).

Seemingly, everybody is online—there are too many wonderful individual Web site and blogs to mention here (but do see our contributors' contact info in their credits). Internet forums are ubiquitous. As mentioned in chapter 4, some of my favorites are: Drawn! (*www.drawn.ca*), IllustrationMundo (*www.illustrationmundo.com*), Sandbox (*www.editoon.com/sandbox*), Cartoon Brew (*www.cartoonbrew.com*), Cartoon Modern (*www.cartoonmodern.blogsome.com*), and YouTube (*www.youtube.com*).

All offer features (or variations) useful to the illustrator: links to artists, plus other content-rich and info-heavy sites; portfolios, samples, and demonstrations (or links to same); discussion groups and chat boards; event notifications and calendars.

Community Center

"Different environments have influenced me, whether it be New York, Los Angeles, or Europe; different professions have as well," says Chris Spollen.

Jenny Kostecki-Shaw wholeheartedly agrees. "My travels to Nepal and India influenced my work greatly," she says, "certainly expanding my color palette, perspective, and views."

We've been making the point that your passion and gusto (for art *and* life) should be without question. But we have also established that you don't have to go it alone. Personal and professional skills flourish in a *community*. The joys and benefits of such a community can spark an illustrator's passion, social skills, and lifestyle.

13
Teach for the Stars

Maybe at times, the saying "Those who can't do, teach" is true. In my experience, I've also seen that "Those who can do, can't teach."

—BILL JAYNES, ILLUSTRATOR

Class Act One common thread running through this book is that a large number of illustrators also teach the art and craft of illustration. It's tempting to say *everybody* teaches. I'd be off, but pretty close.

And I wouldn't say, "It's a surprising fact, but . . ." because this career move makes perfect sense. Teaching is a logical, realistic extension of the practice of illustration.

I diversified early. My entire job history is about the balance of three primary manifestations of my art career: field practice, teaching, and writing. Not coincidentally, the writing thing is a direct result of the first two job descriptions.

Currently, I am primarily a writer and an academic. I only do a minimum number of assignments these days, but my career has always been about the changing ratios of these elements. Like the weather, there will be an inevitable shift somewhere, sometime; I learned to roll with the changes and will do so again.

I have always taught in some capacity and have worked the entire spectrum of art education. I have taught a variety of art disciplines, at every age level (preschool, elementary through post-secondary, and senior citizens as well). For over a decade I've been teaching illustration and graphic design at the college level. Not coincidentally, the teaching thing is an obvious offshoot of the other two job descriptions.

Teaching is exciting. Taxing but satisfying; gratifying yet demanding. Is it hard work? No, it's not a construction job, or brain surgery. Did I mention that the job can be tremendous *fun* at any given moment? And that's without hefting a nail gun or wiping blood and gray matter off your glasses.

Is teaching for you? This chapter will look at many aspects of illustration education and explore the motivations and challenges, frustrations and rewards of this cool gig.

The Debt

For some folks, it's all about carrying it forward. "Certainly, I recognize the need to be a role model and a facilitator for my students demonstrating my passion and devotion to my art, while at the same time communicating as clearly as I can in order to challenge and inspire," says Lampo Leong. "I hope to stimulate my students intellectually, to help them develop a sophisticated taste and a critical eye, and, more importantly, the craving for knowledge."

Leong is not an illustrator per se but *is* a wonderfully creative eclectic immersed in the 2–D format, 3–D genres, and performance and multimedia art. And as it becomes instantly apparent, he absolutely revels in his role as teacher.

He also feels he has an obligation to serve as a link between past and future generations. "The beautiful art of the past, the great art appearing now, the art to which I have dedicated *my life*, was really made by and for people *just like us, and just like our students.*

> *Talking to students revived my passion for the career. I heard myself talking and realized how much I had invested in that career, and how much I knew. I gave my students assignments and drawing exercises that developed me as an illustrator. It was a pivotal experience.*
>
> —LIZZY ROCKWELL, ILLUSTRATOR

"I do my best to assure the liveliness and longevity of the art I love by upholding a standard of teaching that honors discipline as well as creative expression, that rewards effort equally with talent, and that values communication as highly as vision.

"My ultimate wish is to open a path for students that will lead them to discover and actualize their own values," Leong sums up.

Life in the Class Lane

"Right now in my life, I am a full-time teacher, part-time illustrator/ artist," Bill Jaynes states. "From the time I was in college, I knew I wanted to teach illustration/design while being an illustrator at the same time (and I illustrated for about eleven years before I actually began teaching)."

Jaynes cautions that from the outside, teaching looks easy. "My thought was, 'I know this art stuff—I've been to *art school*.' That's when I found out just how *much* work goes into creating and instructing a class.

"You learn that your meticulously prepared lesson plan only covers about half an hour of a three-hour studio. Eight hours looking for the right sample may translate to a mere fifteen minutes of class time. And this doesn't include grading and critiquing or working with students outside of class.

"Then there is the problem of actually finding a way to enable student learning. After being a practicing professional, 'seeing as a beginner' is no easy task. And the focus must be on the students' work, not your own. You're not the star—you become the humble facilitator."

Jaynes wisely (and honestly) points out that balancing an illustration gig with a teaching career is problematic. Perhaps it's because the same type of creative energy fuels both endeavors. "There is a fight for attention much like romancing two lovers at the same time," he muses. "You can end up just tired and heartbroken.

"I've found that art making makes me an authentic teacher in the class-room. During periods where I'm not doing my illustration, the teaching becomes hollow."

WHY TEACH?

So why attempt this tough juggling act? Personally, I teach because the rewards are tremendous.

But don't just take my word for it. "When I first started teaching, it was a way of giving back," says Alex Bostic. "It then grew into a second profession. You have to have something to teach, and I think you should have many years of field experience (as a professional illustrator) before you get into teaching.

"Art is one of those things where you have to *do it* to *really* teach it well," he goes on to say. "To me, it's not so theoretical. You have to be 'in the trade' to know what you are talking about. You have to be in the game."

"Teaching (and working with students) brings a distinct vitality to my life," Bostic continues. "The isolated artist who stays in his shell, enjoying little or no personal contact, often struggles with the outside world.

"I understand my business; I know what to do for the university. I have my routine. It's the students who bring fresh challenges into that mix. Problem–solving for the classroom can cast a new light on the studio. Helping students solve problems helps me solve my problems as well. I see illustration as a constant learning process. So is teaching.

"Students are looking at everything in a new way. To keep up, *you* must also look with that fresh perspective. This forces you to evaluate the state of the art, to appreciate change *and* the here and now. Students want to know *what's going on*, so *I* have to know what's happening to report back. Without a doubt, students are *my* best learning tools."

As an excellent illustrator/professional, how do you transfer your skill and knowledge to another?

—BILL JAYNES, ILLUSTRATOR

WHOSE LEARN IS IT ANYWAY?

Matt McElligott agrees. "I think working with students opens *you* up to new ideas, new approaches, and more. I, too, have discovered that teaching, not surprisingly, has been an excellent education in itself," he asserts. "As anyone who's ever tried it can tell you, there's no better way to really learn something than to try to show someone else how to do it."

"Why do I teach?" David Julian asks the question out loud. "I came into it accidentally, but I love it. I even taught fifth-grade science for a while."

Julian enjoys getting ideas across to people, both verbally and visually. He finds teaching to be a grand combination of these skills: "I like watching people focus on something they haven't seen before and get changed by it." And here, he picks up the thread from McElligott. "I learn from them. In fact, I realize it's a little bit selfish in that I probably teach to learn from other people."

Julian recognizes his teaching to be a great counterbalance and outlet: "It is hard to say who benefits more—the student or the teacher."

I wholeheartedly agree. I've always felt that teaching and learning are two-way streets, for, as Julian appropriately puts it, "You learn as much from the people *you think you are teaching,* whether you're a parent teaching a child or some seasoned career pro teaching a newbie."

"Not many folks are so pompous that they think they teach and don't learn at the same time," Julian sums up. "I can't imagine that they are very good teachers if they're not open to that."

Works for Me

For some, teaching simply rings right. But studio classes are not the only option. Often, illustration instructors teach a derivative topic (a specialty or favorite area of expertise) as part of the curriculum. Business education is one particularly relevant topic; the history of illustration (and general graphic design) is another pertinent extension.

For the teacher, offering a lecture class is a different prep than doing a studio section. Teaching contract writing (or discussing conceptual illustration in the 1950s) is not a hands-on lab experience, like learning how to do a watercolor wash or a scratchboard. So, class organization and structure (overview and investigation; lecture and discussion; Q & A) plus evaluation methods (tests, papers, document writing) will be a different proposition.

As Stan Shaw says, "Teaching allows me to indulge my love of illustration history. The research and reference, combined with my personal, creative experimentation, helps clue *me* into what makes a 'good' or 'successful' illustration. This gives me some insight into how *I* work.

© Stan Shaw

"I also get to see illustration (history and practice) through the eyes of the students—who may or may not be familiar with what makes a good illustration. The constant job of breaking down what I know, taking a good look at it while quantifying for those students, provides a fresh take on this process."

Greg Nemec tells us, "I used to tutor inner-city kids in reading and writing. I was always attracted to igniting that spark of learning. There's a quote that resonates with me here. It goes something like, 'Figure out what you're passionate about and do it, and the money will follow.' However, it took me a long time to figure out that I should be teaching these same kids to make art. So I started art classes for local grade-school kids.

"As an illustrator, I tend to dive into preparation, research, and learning as much as I can before I switch over to the intuitive side and start being creative. I need that foundation to begin.

"With teaching I am less structured. While I always draw from my experience and knowledge, I don't have my entire semester planned out. I don't even always have a month planned out, because I like to see what organically unfolds in the classroom and let that influence what we do next. The same type of thing happens (but at a glacial pace) with my illustration. I didn't plan that this was how my style was going to evolve; one thing just leads to another. Teaching kids has helped me be more open to change and unpredictability in my own work.

"My students are from first grade up to middle school. Classes are in a rented room at a local church. I also teach an animation class at my home. Through flyers and word of mouth, I have a bunch of students who make art with me. The less interested kids have filtered themselves out, so I have enthusiastic students and parents willing to drive them to lessons. Once a week, I also teach at a preschool where art projects feature prominently, and I recently worked with an entire kindergarten class to help them paint a backdrop for their play. I watch these kids draw and paint and wonder which of these younger ones will eventually become my older students."

COME ON IN, THE WATER'S FINE

Isabelle Dervaux is new to teaching. "I was a bit afraid," she admits. "You jump through all these hoops: Maybe I'll have the wrong mix of students; I won't handle it well. I'm out of my league. I'm not cut out for it.

"But friends convinced me otherwise. 'It's fine—just go ahead.' I'm glad I listened to them. I only teach one class for now, but I'm getting a lot out of it.

"For one thing, I'm getting out of the house (something my husband had been pushing me to do). It can be truly lonely being at home all the time. So I felt, 'This is *good*.'

"Belonging to an institution with a solid reputation is great. And school is always buzzing; a lot of things are happening. There are shows, lectures—I feel like a part of something bigger. I see what's going on now and I meet more people (and I think that's really positive). As an illustrator, you have a lot of freedom; you do whatever you want. But at the same time, you need that other connection with the real world.

"Illustrators work so much on their own, you kind of forget how to talk about a problem. You forget how to articulate or think, or how to say something in plain words, logically, *out loud*. Explaining how to make an illustration, you see that what you learned along the way is tremendously valid, that what you're doing is honestly good, and you feel more confident.

"Another thing you'll notice is that you know much more than you think. When I wrote a lesson plan it actually made sense; it even gave *me* a new perspective about the field, like I could have more of a fresh look.

"Teaching enabled me to see that I understand a lot about building an image and what makes a good illustration work (or not). I can discuss style. I can chat about all the different illustrators I've been around. I realize that I've looked at many things and, perhaps most importantly, I discovered that I'm ready to share it now. I've discovered I'm *excited* to share it now!

"My enthusiasm was way up," Dervaux informs. "If I taught a night class, the next day I'd be on kind of a high. *I did it*. I overcame the challenges of public speaking!" She laughs.

"I didn't expect to really enjoy the teaching part, but I actually loved the connection. I had adult students who were eager and interesting and ready to learn. They asked the right questions. A few of my students were incredibly talented.

"All in all, it was pretty satisfying, " Dervaux concludes. "Maybe in ten years it won't be, but so far, so good."

Job Hunt

If you are interested in teaching, how do you begin to build those opportunities?

One obvious answer is to attend an accredited institution, get your degree (and certification), and look for teaching jobs. A bachelor's degree should enable you to teach studio classes at the community college level; you'll need state certification to do kindergarten through twelfth-grade art.

You'll need a master's degree to teach in programs that offer a bachelor's degree. Depending on the place and program, the requirement will be an MA or an MFA. The hiring committee will also look hard at your art (of course) and professional experience.

What if your field experience is wonderful, your work obviously superior, but you just don't have the teaching credentials? Depending on guidelines and need, a local school *may* be able to bend the rules if your résumé is not quite up to speed. There are no guarantees here (certification is in place for a good reason), but it's not so unusual. For instance, you could be paired with another instructor/mentor in a team-teaching situation. The accredited prof will be the teacher of record; you will co-teach as an "artist in residence."

Speaking of which, artist-in-residence programs are a great segue into the classroom. Investigate public and private schools that offer this agenda. Research arts councils and centers. Check the phone book for local contact info; head to the library's reference section for names, numbers, and addresses outside your area.

Also consider teaching classes for those same schools, arts councils, and centers (as well as the YMCA). These organizations offer fine teaching opportunities year round. Semesters usually sync with the school year (don't forget summer art camps, either). Give (public, private, and post-secondary) school seminars. Offer private classes. Do workshops at libraries and senior centers.

A simple idea, really. Build your résumé of teaching experience and move up the academic ladder.

For Whom the School Bell Tolls

It bears repeating: Teaching is a fun, exciting gig. It's a gratifying occupation that will demand a serious investment of your expertise, time, and energy. Teaching is no mere grunt job. You can't "phone it in." You won't get rich (quick or otherwise). The rewards (and they are substantial) are elsewhere.

And I'll ask the question again: Is teaching for you? Remember, teaching is a calling that truly is in a class by itself.

14
Outside
the Art Box

*I never thought of illustration as the
most important thing in life. My priorities
have always been my dog, my husband,
and then my work.*

—VIVIENNE FLESHER, ILLUSTRATOR

Dealing with Change   If all goes well, at some ripe old age, you will
quietly keel over at the drawing table. You'll leave a backlog of assignments
(that your kid, the rock–star illustrator, will finish). The industry—no,
mankind in general—will celebrate a noted life, praise your considerable talents, and mourn your passage to that great lightbox in the sky.

But sometimes blips on your professional and/or personal radar mean
learning to rethink the wisdom of, and maybe evaluating alternatives to, what
you are doing. We wield no true control of our lives (or career). The only real
say we have is in how we deal with the realities of life and business.

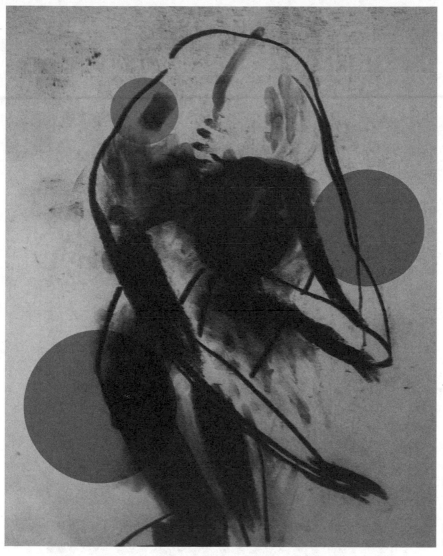

© Vivienne Flesher

This chapter is about decisions. It's about the glory of transitions and the benefits of weighing alternatives. It's about moving on: what to do during dry spells, what's truly important at various stages in your career, or what to do when things go south or sour (which can mean moving in and out of the illustration field, or even leaving the fold entirely).

Everything Changes

Like many folks, Ward Schumaker has worked in a variety of fields, but he tells us he didn't begin his illustration career until he was thirty-five. "I quit being a paper salesman to become a designer," he says, "and then switched from that into illustration.

"I'd always meant to become a fine artist but never pulled it off. I was raised to think that only fine art was important—illustration was nothing—and I subscribed to that idea, even though I always had questions about the relevance of fine art. Still, it's more my passion.

"You have to figure out what's important in life. Is art important, or is it something else? And if you're like a lot of people, you'll fight about it in your head. Not worrying about such things will allow you to go a lot further. Unfortunately, my thoughts about this subject are still a muddle.

"Yet I should also say how much I truly admire illustrators. It's amazing that people can sit in their studio and jump to it—create an illustration just because someone else has asked them for something—and produce such wonderful results. To think that people can adapt so quickly to someone else's needs and express that visually—well, that's really impressive. I'm so impressed with so many illustrators.

"And this is the life! You don't have to talk to anybody much. You can just sit there and draw pictures! Make delivery and send a bill!

"There was a time where I could turn work down and still work twelve to fourteen hours, seven days a week," Schumaker remembers. "Sorry to say, it's not like that now. I don't know how many people are actually earning a good living as illustrators today."

Creative Alternatives

"Illustrators *are* struggling," Vivienne Flesher agrees, "and I don't think it's for lack of trying."

Flesher admits she hasn't been working so much these last years, but it's actually been a very creative time for her. "I spent a lot of the time just experimenting (and getting enough work so that I wasn't panicking about bills). But I'm certainly not getting as much work as I'd like, which means I'm not creating as many paintings as I would like."

At the beginning of her career, Flesher was fortunate to get work right away. But in doing so, she felt typecast. She confesses, "I couldn't break out of it. My work stayed the same throughout that time. But I was able to make it evolve, and I'm having so much fun doing what I'm doing now. I had a great time. I took a lot of photographs, learned how to use the computer, learned how to use a digital camera."

Seizing the Moment

"When the slowdown began, we all felt like, 'Oh my God, why am I failing?'" Flesher reflects. "Is my style *out* of style? Maybe if I had two or three different ways of drawing, I could weather this period better."

And that's exactly what she did. By resolving to fully use the time *and enjoy it*, Flesher decided to seize that moment. "Too many of my friends were getting upset and anxious about it. I just felt like being constructive instead of destructive. I thought I'd just try to do some of the things that I'd always wanted to do.

"I had enough savings so that we could last for a while, and I was making enough to pay the bills and still put some money away. But it was obvious that things really changed.

"It's surprising which folks are in this predicament. And I think they're taking all of this way too personally," she says. And here, Flesher says with a laugh, "Maybe it's a guy thing—they just feel they should be doing something more. And women have always thought, 'God, there are so many things to accomplish!'"

Could've, should've, didn't, wouldn't. Can't, and don't, and maybe not. Are these big buzzwords in your daily vocabulary?

© Anthony Freda

"There are too many whiners out there," Loughran comments. "Don't complain that work's not happening. The way to change things isn't to complain. Get motivated!

"Look for opportunities; pursue them—*make* something happen. Create opportunities for yourself or seek them out. The world doesn't *need* more illustrators. There's no lack of talent. If anything, there's a lack of discipline and ambition."

Going Down?

What do you do when your business appears to be going under?

The first thing I would do is consult your accountant. If you don't have one, get one. Spend the money.

Ask your accountant what financial records she needs to see, and from how many years back. Most likely, this will encompass the documentation of both past and present income and expenditures and will include all relevant tax returns. You want this objective professional to paint a tangible picture of the *viability* of your business based on your financial history (and present situation). Gather up the paperwork, go with an open mind, and ask for straight information and honest answers.

This works both ways. Be completely honest with the accountant about how you do business. There will be reasons why your business is going belly-up, and *you are involved.*

Ask your accountant what it will take to stay in business—what you have to earn to make ends meet. But here's the deal: You shouldn't slave to just "get by," and you shouldn't remain in business to only break even.

"But I love drawing. I love being an illustrator!" you protest. Okay. It's one thing if it's just you, and you don't mind mac and cheese at the Mac

---

every night. But the world of bills and spills must make you consider the practicality of being in the illustration *business*.

So now look at that business. What jobs are coming in? What kind of work are you getting? How much work is coming in? What does your next week look like . . . your next month . . . this quarter?

How much do these jobs bring in? What's the pay schedule on these gigs? How's your cash flow? Does the math make or mock the budget your accountant says you need to stay afloat, to turn a profit, to buy that yacht?

I wouldn't give up without a fight. Go to the library. Read and research all the business material you can. (There is a ton of stuff about all aspects of staying in business.) Hit the Internet. Same thing here: Research, research, research. There is a world of business info online. Don't believe everything you read (or find), but be open to what resonates for you particularly.

Network. Call your arty colleagues and talk to your non-arty friends. Go back online. Most illustration organizations and communities (plus many individual sites or blogs) have business-focused chat rooms, forums, and interviews. Read existing pertinent content. If you're comfortable laying it out there, participate. Start a new thread; ask specific questions.

Again, don't buy it all. Everyone's an expert on the Internet. Everyone has considerable opinions, and it's always open-mic night.

Make your list and check it twice. Absorb what will work best for you. Now, come up with an action plan to make your business fly higher (see chapters 5, 7, 8, 11, and 12 of this book for more on all this).

Change the way you do business—or move on gracefully. And to the best of your ability: No judgments, no guilt—that's all part of the action plan, too. Don't let anything get in the way of the ultimate goals: Do it better and/or do it different.

Attitude

The empowerment PJ Loughran advocates provides a huge sense of his daily worth. If things go well or head south, he's responsible. This is not an Olympian trait; it's within all of us. It's that balance and control that makes the difference.

For many illustrators, "taking it personally" just means personally taking it in a positive direction. You can succumb to the hard knocks, or look at a downturn as the trumpet call to charge. Either way, you'll have to approach your challenges from the left or right of that center.

"It makes sense to explore. Change is refreshing," Mike Quon says. "My career dream was to be a designer and an illustrator. I realized that dream by working almost continuously, juggling the creative side with a heavy dose of promotion and marketing. But when my design and illustration business grew to where I was spending more time selling and managing than I was creating or working on other parts of my life, I realized it was time to downsize.

"Whether it was having a smaller shop or just the perceived 'downturn' in the industry, a less consuming work life made it possible for me to start a family and do all the things that go along with having kids and a home life," Quon continues. "I still count illustration as a good part of my business, but I've adjusted my time to make room for other things as well, like teaching an illustration course at a local college and really focusing on my logo work.

"Illustrators in general have a tendency to be a bit obsessed. You know, before it was just me and the job. Now, making a living, raising a family, and getting work done—it is all juggling. It's a different ball game; I have to make every minute of my working hours count.

I think this notion that editorial illustration is dead is flat-out false. But if interest wanes, you have to evolve, or do something else. Go with the flow or step off.

—PJ LOUGHRAN, ILLUSTRATOR

"A new approach to work can help you answer some tough questions about what you really want your life to be about," Quon advises. "What is success? What do you really want? For me, it was realizing that raising children was my biggest design project—too big to miss.

"So, go for the proverbial brass ring. Take the chances. But have the 'nerve' to move on to something else (big or small). Keep moving, learning, and making adjustments; keep fine-tuning it. Remember, it's all an experiment anyway. And it is about the journey as much as it is about the destination.

"Sometimes I think it would be fun if there were some 'creative law' that required us to change our careers halfway through. I am not telling you to get out of illustration, but I know an illustrator who is also an aromatherapist, and a fine artist who owns a delicatessen. If you have to work another job to supplement your income, so be it. Maybe this makes you become a more interesting person, and it's just another chapter in your life story.

"Remember, it is about creativity. Creating keeps you evolving in so many different ways. It *might* mean doing something new, instead of the same thing you have been doing for all those many years. What a concept! Just make sure you are doing enough of what you want."

Inspection

Whether you are just starting out as an illustrator, in midcareer (or further), it's always a good idea to periodically evaluate your professional life, and to make changes if, and as, necessary.

So, reader, how do you tap into this good advice? Empowerment, as Loughran points out, equates to responsibility. You begin the process by examining directions, both positive and negative. What creative strategy really clicked lately? (Please remember, "lately" is relative.) What flopped? Any ideas or concrete information why on either count?

Rousing success stories, hard-knock tales, positive trends, or down-turns will signal a future tactic. Change, as Quon said, can be quite inspirational—one way or another. What inspires you—to do what, and how?

Inspiration sparks choices. Evaluation breeds answers. Don't duck the tough questions (or avoid risks); *embrace* the change Quon mentions. Own your transformations, your way.

Outlook

Your dad was right: Failure or disappointment is a learning experience. And your mom was right on the money: Even though you crave a challenge, you must live in the present. If a job is beyond your skill set, it's okay to turn it down. It's fine to enjoy a modest enterprise, which goes back to Quon's earlier point: "What do you want? What business are you in? What types of projects will make you happy?" And, as Quon wisely points out, "Do be careful what you wish for. You just might get it."

Art-Related Employment

"I think illustration is a great hobby," Flesher states, "but you need a day job or something else—or five other things. Teaching, writing; that whole spirit of being an entrepreneur. Use your gifts. A lot of illustrators have taken other jobs just because they're not making enough money."

Charlene Smith works in the trend department for Target Corporation. "At Target, I research trends to see what's new, and how current color and design affects our product. I guide the overall *look and feel* and have to be aware of the big picture."

As a student, did Smith envision she'd be where she is now? "I thought I was going to do freelance editorial illustration," she remembers. "I'm finding now, as I go back and talk to students, that *this is what everybody thinks* they're going to do. If they find success in it, great, but that's a *big* hurdle for someone just out of school."

And here, Smith smiles and says, "You know, my dad still laughs when he remembers me saying, 'I'm going to art school.' Dad, being a trooper, did *not* respond with, 'You're going to have a job, right? You're not going to be living on the street?'

"Now that I *do* have a nine-to-five job which allows me to travel (and other great perks), Dad is the *spokesperson* for art education. So, art school is more than weird hair, people hanging out, and suspected drug abuse. You can come out of it with a *real* career.

"But I didn't even know *this* was a bona fide career path," Smith comments about her work at Target. "I was on an internship for a designer who saw that I was doing a lot of pattern collage. She asked if I ever thought about doing surface design, and I wondered out loud, 'What exactly is *that*?' I had no clue. I didn't know such a job even existed.

"This design consultant recommended Target Corporation and gave me the name of her contact. I checked it out, and ended up doing an internship there (and ultimately working full-time, on staff)."

Non-Art Employment and the "Ultimate Solution"

"We know life's not fair. There are a lot of talented folks not making enough money," Quon says flatly.

"I know a designer who works at Home Depot in the evenings to make ends meet. So be it. This is a discouraging story to me *only if he stops making art* due to this outside employment. Honest work, if done because it's part of your action plan, is just part of keeping the machine moving forward."

I agree with Quon wholeheartedly. Keeping diapers on the baby, putting food on the table—getting all the ends to meet honestly—only makes you a big mensch in my book.

© Susanna Pitzer

Branching Out

To sum up, I'll capsulize a story told to me by John Dykes. Dykes attended a lecture given by Maurice Sendak, who discussed two different types of artists. One knew exactly what he wanted and went right after it. The other artistic type didn't know; he tried a bit of this, going here and there, but always branching. For Sendak, the second artist was the hands-down favorite.

Dykes's Sendak story resonates with me. So, let me add my take here. You may have to branch off. You might be forced to go out on a different limb.

And even if it doesn't have artistic roots, this act is still a responsible (and responsive) effort of grace, wit, and style.

Go for it, and keep your head up.

Other Avenues

What are some different paths you might explore in terms of non–illustration jobs? Besides teaching, are there other avenues that can offer you financial and creative fulfillment?

Yep. Sure! Think about arts administration (for instance, run or work at an arts council). Or creative consulting (do the lecture, workshop, and seminar circuit). Many folks I know have a closet dream of running an art store (a bit like owning the candy shop).

How about working in an art gallery, even starting a bookstore (art, comics, and/or otherwise)? I know artists who manufacture (or import) and sell artful gadgets and items online—even brick and mortar.

You can brainstorm this as well as I can. The point is that, should it come to this, a non–illustration job does not have to be boring and mind-numbing. Besides, you haven't quit drawing and painting, have you?

15
Some Ties That Bind

Allow yourself to gravitate to, rather than aim specifically at, something. You will crash land otherwise.

—PAUL DALLAS, ILLUSTRATOR
    AND EDUCATOR

Connections   In my mind's eye, when I picture the practice of illustration, I visualize substantial links in an extensive chain, or interwoven strands of a rich and sturdy fabric. This chapter is about those connections.

On one level is the thread of history—the continuum of illustration. We are indeed the product of our inspirations, our concentrated study (and casual reference), and, of course, our teachers. I have a reverence for this particular thread, the fabric of process that weaves the eras of illustration together, and I believe we're charged with paying that forward. As a teacher (and a colleague), I try to do my bit here.

At another level is the collective society of illustration. Not just some grandiose notion, the global community is a true reality, linked by communication and delivery systems that have never been faster and easier, more efficient, more fun.

On a related tier is the state of the art. Let's consider technology: the advancement of the science (and craft) of illustration. I've always been into the stuff of my profession; we get to play with a lot of joyful tools and toys.

> *There is a reason artists used to copy the masters to learn. Their work still teaches us.*
>
> —ERIN BRADY WORSHAM, ILLUSTRATOR

I can't say I was a pioneer, but I was a digital convert early. But what's sweet is that, as a kid, I felt the same rush cracking open a box of sixty-four crayons (with the sharpener, of course). Later, buying my first fax machine—and that first fax transmission—was *magic*.

A World View

"As an artist with an inspired imagination, I feel I enjoy my world in a special and unique way," says Federico Jordán. "But perhaps this is a bit immodest, or somewhat pretentious," he wonders.

Jordán lives and works in Monterrey, Mexico, and admits he sometimes questions how his world would look through another's eyes. "Is it all so wonderful from others' perspectives? One's culture shapes you (as well as being a reflection of who you are). As an illustrator, I want to understand that 'whole world of differences,' while still looking at it from my point of view—and get this down in my work.

"Every culture has a certain spirit," Jordán says. "Understanding this will take me right to the target. I think that communication is the essence of our craft. Communication—that's really the ability to look through another's eyes."

> *Be mindful of what you don't want to do, perhaps more than what you want to do.*
>
> —PAUL DALLAS, ILLUSTRATOR AND EDUCATOR

And in San Francisco, illustrator Ward Schumaker agrees. "That communication is now truly global," he comments. "Which is a big difference from when I began as an illustrator. It's a much smaller world.

"The world is really just one big conversation, and an illustrator communicates visually the stories people are telling each other. Illustration helps snag readers, whether it's through concept or narrative or style: You look at an illustration, and if the concept or narrative interests you and the style suggests your particular group (or a group you aspire to), you want to read that article or that magazine. An illustrator helps pass ideas around."

I REMEMBER YOU

We all want to leave some kind of legacy, to make our mark, to have made a difference. For you—personally or professionally—the jury may still be out on the above questions, but as Rick Sealock suggests, "It may be more reasonable to ask what *not* to be remembered for."

He clarifies what he means here: "Don't be boring, don't be safe, don't be a sellout, don't be a suck on society, and don't proliferate 'bad' aesthetics," Sealock emphasizes. "If you are in it for the money, then so be it—but don't ever pretend you are educating or advancing the level of current illustration.

And each to his own. It's all about the letter 'i'. Strive to be innovative, interesting, and introspective."

Comin' Around Again

Sam Viviano recalls his dad's oft-used comment that "there's nothing new under the sun." And from the vantage point of somebody who's been doing this a long time—almost thirty years—Viviano has been very conscious of this in illustration as well as in other art forms. "Music, for instance," he tells you. "I tend to hear more of the influences on the artist rather than the song itself, because it is absolutely true that none of us works in a vacuum. We are part of that continuum you mention before.

"And illustrators are part of the stream of art," Viviano goes on to say. "I think it's literally impossible to communicate—to express yourself—without tools that have been long passed down."

"There is a lineage and an inherited quality in illustration," Bill Russell says. "This is a wonderful thing. I had teachers [at Parsons] like David Passalacqua, who always talked about great graphics in a drawing. Passalacqua would show his teachers' work, specifically Rico LeBrun, and I carried that through when I taught—I would show Dave's work, and how it influenced me. I think students love that, knowing that they are part of a history.

The changing paradigms of art run parallel to scientific evolution. In this new information age, new technologies play an ever more important role in education, offering a wealth of alternative ways for students to access and integrate new theoretical concepts into their reservoirs of practical knowledge. For instance, combining both text and images, in all sorts of creative and interactive formats, makes for an enjoyable and stimulating learning experience.
—LAMPO LEONG, ARTIST AND EDUCATOR

"We as illustrators keep trying to create something unique," Russell continues. "Yes, that's a good thing, but when I look at a drawing by Brad Holland, I can't not think about Goya's 'The Disasters of War' prints. The history of illustration—that heritage of illustration—is vital."

Well, in light of that, ask yourself how important it is for *you* to know something (or anything) about illustration history.

"The most original, creative, and extensive career illustrators have an amazing knowledge of the history of illustration and fine art," Sealock states in support of Viviano's above premise. "For one to see any new influences or fads in illustration, one only has to look back at the history of these fields."

Coda

It is fitting for the final chapter of this book (as well as the conclusion of both the chapter and the book itself) to be about *connections*.

Your connection to the past, present, and future of illustration—surely other artists, and definitely the process of communication—is what being an illustrator is all about. Being an artist (and growing as an illustrator) is about making those connections.

Erin Brady Worsham says it well: "As artists, we can't know where we're going until we've seen where we've been." To that I would add, "You don't know who you are until you recognize and interact with your community." Process and technique? I'm assuming you are simply an *amazing* artist (and I'd bet I'm right, one way or another).

History, inspiration; practice, reference, and study; thinking it through (and yes, process, of course)—that's "school." The campus is global; our communications and technology are advanced. The state of the art, as a direct result? Just fine, thank you.

I'm not lamenting (or grousing about) the state of the *business*; there's plenty of opportunity to do that (and certainly, if we pay attention to the aforementioned connections, we'll also find the manpower, time, and commitment to do something about it).

Here, I just want you to consider where we've been, where we are, and where we're going. Or maybe I should say, where we're *growing*—because that will keep those connections vital. Be well connected and grow.

I'm a lucky guy—I have always had a direction. Not a particularly motivated student, and definitely no football hero, I rock-and-rolled through high school and college. But mostly there was ART (in big, capital letters mind you . . . is there any other way to do it?) The goal was always to do exactly what I'm doing now, and I pulled it off.

I have my passions, two of which are making art and the practice of art education. I have a BA in Art Ed, and an MA in painting and drawing from Indiana University of Pennsylvania. I love to teach art, and I've worked with every age level, from preschoolers to senior citizens. For the last 6 years, I've taught graphic design, illustration, and fine arts at Edison Community College, where I am also Program and Staffing Coordinator.

My writing is the direct offspring of my illustration career. I wouldn't have predicted that I'd be a writer, but here I am and it's a great gig.

How To Grow As An Illustrator is my second book for Allworth Press. Exploring Illustration was recently published and I'm currently developing a new series called The Visual Artist At Work. I've also written for a variety of publications including How Magazine, Step Inside Design magazine, Computer Arts Projects (UK), and more.

I was a featured presenter at DesignWorld (How's annual conference, in 2002), the NISOD annual conference in 2004 where I was awarded a national teaching excellence award, and ICON 4 in 2005.

I live in Yellow Springs, Ohio, where I scored some of my first illustration gigs twenty-five years ago. I am married to the award-winning documentary filmmaker, Joanne Caputo—easily the most beautiful woman in any room—and the father of Max (16), and Cooper (19).

—MICHAEL FLEISHMAN

Index

Books from Allworth Press

Allworth Press is an imprint of Allworth Communications, Inc. Selected titles are listed below.

Starting Your Career as a Freelance Illustrator or Graphic Designer, Revised Edition
by Michael Fleishman (paperback, 6 × 9, 272 pages, $19.95)

Inside the Business of Illustration
by Steven Heller and Marshall Arisman (paperback, 6 × 9, 256 pages, $19.95)

Business and Legal Forms for Illustrators, Third Edition
by Tad Crawford (paperback, 8½ × 11, 160 pages, $29.95)

The Education of an Illustrator
edited by Steven Heller and Marshall Arisman (paperback, 6¾ × 9⅞, 288 pages, $19.95)

Teaching Illustration: Course Offerings and Class Projects from the Leading Undergraduate and Graduate Programs
edited by Steven Heller and Marshall Arisman (paperback, 6 × 9, 288 pages, $19.95)

Your Career in Animation: How to Survive and Thrive
by David B. Levy (paperback, 6 × 9, 256 pages, $19.95)

Animation: The Whole Story, Revised Edition
by Howard Beckerman (paperback, 6⅞ × 9¾, 336 pages, $24.95)

The Education of a Comics Artist
by Michael Dooley and Steven Heller (paperback, 6 × 9, 288 pages, $19.95)

The Business of Being an Artist, Third Edition
by Daniel Grant (paperback, 6 × 9, 352 pages, $19.95)

Legal Guide for the Visual Artist, Fourth Edition
by Tad Crawford (paperback, 8½ × 11, 272 pages, $19.95)

Licensing Art and Design, Revised Edition
by Caryn R. Leland (paperback, 6 × 9, 128 pages, $16.95)

Successful Syndication: A Guide for Writers and Cartoonists
by Michael Sedge (paperback, 6 × 9, 192 pages, $16.95)

Mastering 3D Animation, Second Edition with CD-ROM
by Peter Ratner (paperback, 8 × 9⅞, 352 pages, $40.00)